D0981610

Pastors Need Prayer:

Holding up Your Pastor's Arms through Prayer

by Ted Rose

World Press Publishing
Grandville, MI

Unless otherwise indicated, all scripture quotations are taken from the King James Version of the Bible.

PASTORS NEED PRAYER:
ISBN 13: 978-1492112471
ISBN 10: 149211247X
Holding up your Pastor's arms through Prayer
Copyright @ 2013 by Ted Rose
United States National Prayer Council
P.O. Box 52
Carmichael, CA 95609

Published by World Press Publishing

Endorsements from Christian Leaders

Dr. Luis Palau

President and Founder of the Luis Palau Evangelistic Association

"Ted Rose doesn't just write about the importance of prayer, he lives his life as a powerful and transparent example. I had the privilege of serving with Ted in 2012 during a major evangelistic campaign in Northern California. Ted was our Co-Chair of the Prayer Committee for the Sacramento City Festival where many thousands came to Christ. It was there where I learned of his passionate commitment to the Lord, to prayer, and to the local church. His testimony was a blessing to me, and I know this book will be a blessing to many more. Pastors, this is a must read for everyone of your church members- Pastors Need Prayer."

Dave Butts

Chairman of America's National Prayer Committee
President of Harvest Prayer Ministries

"Ted Rose has gotten right to the heart of one of the great crises in the Church today and has handled it with grace and power. This book, 'Pastors Need Prayer,' is a clarion call to pray for pastors. He not only tells us that we ought to, but shows us how in very practical ways."

Mike Bickle

Director of the International House of Prayer in Kansas City and Leader to the Prayer Movement of Houses of Prayer across the world

"This book, 'Pastors Need Prayer' by Ted Rose, will be a valuable tool to the Body of Christ! My prayer is that it will birth a passion in you to pray for your pastor as never before. I believe that this book will stir the call to prayer and give you understanding of why it's so needed. Though your prayers, you have an opportunity to profoundly affect your church and its total ministry."

Rev. H.B. London
Called "America's Pastor to Pastors"
Founder of "Pastor to Pastor at Focus on the Family"
Founder of Pastor/Clergy Appreciation Month, observed worldwide.

"Ted Rose absolutely has one of the deepest loves for pastors that I know of. His understanding of their needs, as well as the genuine call of God upon him, propels him to lay down his own life in hour upon hour of intercession on their behalf. This book will inspire you in its direct instruction of how to serve your pastor in prayer. I wholeheartedly endorse this book, 'Pastors Need Prayer,' to every believer."

R.T. Kendall
Former Pastor of Westminster Chapel in England
One of the most influential Pastors of our generation

"This book is packed with the strategic prayer experience of Ted Rose, a 30+ year intercessor! 'Pastor's Need Prayer' is a must read for all who value your pastor in the high calling of shepherding real-life people in today's real-life world."

Suzette Hattingh
Former Director of Intercession for Reinhard Bonnke's ministry for 16 years.
President and Director of Voice in the City

"This book will challenge your heart as its content moves from the inner heart of one intercessor to the outward expression of prayer, against the schemes of the enemy forged against your pastor/leader. As one intercessor is joined by another, and then another, on behalf of their leadership, we will see the enemy greatly defeated and church/work of God, increasingly victorious in every City, State and Nation. I endorse this book by Pastor Ted Rose, and encourage you to read it and make an impact where God has positioned you!"

Eddie & Alice Smith
Founders of U.S. Prayer Center, in Houston, Texas
President and Executive Director of Eddie and Alice Smith Minitries

"Perhaps no one we know is better equipped than Ted to have written this important book, 'Pastors Need Prayer.' Ted, the son of a pastor, was reared in a pastor's home. He has spent his life in Christian ministry and knows first- hand what enormous physical, emotional and spiritual pressures are brought to bear on pastors and their families. He knows the vital importance of ministers and ministries being shielded by the prayers of God's faithful intercessors. Pastor, this book will help you understand much of that which you've been struggling, and why. Praying Christians, this book will reveal a prayer ministry that has for too long remained hidden and unfulfilled. Get it. Read it. Do it."

Nancy McDaniel

International Director of Prayer for Aglow International

"Ted Rose carries the heart and insight for praying for our pastors in a passionate and loving way. Pastors face extraordinary challenges to nurture and lead the church in this unique time of God's unfolding plan for His Kingdom. This book should be read by every Christian and intercessor who truly wants to pray effectively for pastors and people in ministry. Prepare to gain insight and impartation! Prepare to see our pastors empowered, encouraged, and enlarged."

Karen Covell
Director and Founder of the Hollywood Prayer Network

'Pastors Need Prayer'. What a truthful statement that needs to be shouted out from the mountaintops. Ted Rose has approached a much needed issue head on, and every church-goer should read this book. When I ask my closest pastor friend how he's doing, he often says, 'I'm doing my best, but I'm still full of sheep bites!' So, let's embrace Ted's message and not complain to our pastors, demand things from them, or expect them to act and be a certain way. But let's pray for them and watch how the Lord will bless and honor them, and grow the church. Thank you Ted, for challenging all of us to be a part of the solution."

Ed Moore
Senator Ed Moore (OK-Ret)
President, Prayer Force One

"Any work that brings pastor and flock closer together is a worthy work, and nobody does it better than Ted Rose. The Bible says, "Smite the shepherd and the sheep shall be scattered." (Zach.13:7) Ted's book will prevent this from happening so that both shepherd and flock are greatly benefited. Every Christian should read this book!"

T.C. Kim
National Coordinator Transform World USA

"Indeed the enemies bull's eye target is placed directly on the pastor to weaken and disarm the church, leave them powerless in slumber. Jesus said the gates of hell shall not prevail against His church. The Enemy's only enemy is the church. The Church has been given the same authority and power of Jesus, by Jesus. The intercessory prayers of the congregation will be the iron wall which the enemy's arrow of fire could not break through. Our Lord may question each of the churches congregation for their fallen pastor at the Judgment Seat. This strategic awakening may arise from every church in the USA through this important book "Pastors Need Prayer" by Pastor Ted Rose."

Rev. Mark Gonzales
Founder United States Hispanic Prayer Network
and Hispanic Action Network

Like every Moses needs an Aaron and Hur...so too does every pastor need a praying people holding him up to accomplish what God has called him to do here on the earth!!!

This book is an insightful look into the life and calling of pastors. Your pastor and the role you play as his flock and intercessors in the success or failure of his ministry and calling.

The office of pastor in our current society is not what it use to be. The challenges are greater then they have ever been in the history of the church. (There is a reason why insurance policies want to know if you are a pastor, and if so your rates go up.) It is considered one of the most stressful occupations in society today.

If there is any one alive today that needs your prayers like never before it's your pastor. From the seasoned intercessor to the brand new believer, everyone needs and has a responsibility to pray for their pastor.

Our prayer is that you will be challenged to action and not just being a church attender, but become a prayer warrior for your pastor. Pastors Need Prayer is a must read for every member that occupies and sits in a pew in any church anywhere. After you read this book, you will never look at your pastor the same way again.

Phil Miglioratti
Facilitator National Pastors Prayer Network
Church Prayer Leaders Network

"The Body of Christ has been blessed by the faithful prayer ministry of Ted Rose, especially for pastors. I endorse the book, 'Pastors Need Prayer' and I intend to encourage the pastors and intercessors of the National Pastors' Prayer Network (NPPN.org) and Pray! Network (Praynetwork.org) to not only learn new insights and ideas from this book, but to use it to teach and train many others as well."

Pastor Wally Magdangal
North America Director
of International Day of Prayer for the Persecuted
Church.
Senior Pastor of The Gathering

"In his book, 'Pastors Need Prayer: Holding up Your Pastor's Arms through Prayer,' Ted Rose convincingly presents a challenge for every follower of Christ, to seriously pray for their pastors. Ted Rose has a loving and tender concern for every pastor. If only Christians will begin to pray for their pastors, revival will break out, demons will tremble, and the church will be able to fulfill God's mandate. Churches across America and beyond need to make this book available to their congregations."

Dr. Che Ahn
Senior Pastor of HRock Church
President of Harvest International Ministry,
An international network of more than 150 churches.

"Pastors have been given an enormous responsibility to care, nurture, teach, and disciple their congregation. They receive vision and direction for the church God has given them to lead and the community He's called them to reach. Ultimately Pastors are accountable to God for shepherding His sheep. With this calling comes spiritual warfare that can manifest in so many ways and over time become debilitating and discouraging. Pastor Ted Rose, also an avid intercessor for pastors, has written a powerful book 'Pastors Need Prayer' Holding up Your Pastor's Arms through Prayer." I highly recommend this must read book which provides you with strategic and effective keys to keep your pastor covered and protected through prayer and intercession."

Pastor Jim Franklin
Senior Pastor of Cornerstone Church

"If there ever was a man of prayer, Ted Rose is that man. He first shared the principles contained within this book 'Pastors Need Prayer' with my leadership over two decades ago, it revolutionized our church. For the first time people began to understand how important it was to pray for their pastor. Plus he equipped them with practical steps to accomplish this most necessary exercise. This is a book that every member of the body of Christ needs to read."

Pastor Dennis McGuire
Senior Pastor of Acata First Baptist Church

"I have known Ted Rose for approximately 25 years as a friend, fellow servant and faithful intercessor on behalf of the Body of Christ. I am also honored to have served as Ted's pastor and had the privilege of our church sending him out to start a strategic Prayer ministry in Sacramento, CA. that continues to this day, some 20+ years later. For as long as I have known Ted ,he has had a passion for prayer and a call to teach and equip the Church in the area of intercession. In my estimation, Ted is a present day Apostle of Prayer. I know for a fact that this book is a small reflection of a life of prayer and the overflow of a person that has lived out the principles of this book for at least 3 decades of ministry to the Body of Christ. I could not recommend more highly 'Pastor's Need Prayer'. This book is an urgent and needed message to the Church regarding the realities that are facing those men and woman of God that serve in pastoral roles in the Church. 'Pastors Need Prayer' not only addresses the challenges every pastor faces but also provides profound inspiration and practical instruction on how a church can cover their pastor(s) in prayer. **I do not exaggerate when I say that there may not be a more important book or more urgent of a message than that which exists within the pages of this book.**"

Pastor Roderick Gittens
Senior Pastor of San Francisco Christian Center

"I was excited to see a book that addressed an important issue in the Body of Christ that can go unnoticed, and that is the need for prayer for pastors. Ted Rose strategically addresses one of the key elements that the Body of Christ in America and around the world will greatly benefit from, and that is praying for our pastors. This book shows that prayer is the most powerful weapon that we have as believers, but the most seldom used. But as believers begin to unleash the power of prayer for pastors, the church will greatly advance the Kingdom of God in challenging times. I believe this book will be an excellent teaching tool for church leaders and members alike. I highly recommend and endorse 'Pastors Need Prayer'"

Pastor Brad Alford
Senior Pastor of New Day Church

"As a Pastor, nothing impacts my church more than a praying people. When I met Ted Rose and had him come, he imparted to us a spirit of prayer that brought us to another level of power and authority. He showed to my church the importance and urgency of praying for their Pastor and leaders!

Revelation and understanding came to us that continues to change our lives!

I have known Ted Rose for years now and feel like I have known him for decades!! He carries the heart and passion of Christ who himself daily intercedes for us. This book is a must read for intercessors and prayer warriors who are on the front lines fighting in prayer. Pastors need prayer: if the head is defeated, so will the body be. If the head is weak, so will the body be. As the scripture says, **"Strike the Shepherd and the sheep will scatter!" But this book 'strikes' back at the evil plans of the enemy and does a masterful job in demolishing demonic devices!!** Great pastors are men and women who have great prayer lifted up to heaven on their behalf! Thanks Ted for writing such a timely book!"

Pastor Francis Anfuso
Senior Pastor of The Rock Church of Roseville

"Is there any more important relationship that needs to be restored than the bond between a pastor and an intercessor? What power remains untapped until these vital ministries are united as one? Like Frodo and Samwise in Tolkien's "The Lord of the Rings," Sam, as a faithful armor bearer, is willing to give his life so that Frodo's mission is completed. Ted Rose captures this critical connection in his groundbreaking book 'Pastor's Need Prayer.' As a pastor, I have found that my life would not be safe, and my ministry could not be fulfilled without the faithful intercession of dedicated prayer warriors. Ted Rose has been just that, and now offers his priceless insights to others."

Dedication

I would like to dedicate this book and acknowledge very special people who have made it possible to fulfill the vision of God throughout my years of ministry:

First, I want to thank my amazing and beautiful wife, Dee Rose. Dee, you are the love of my life. Also, I want to thank my son Teddy. I am so proud of you son. And thank you, my sweet daughter Tiffany, you are a great gift from God to your mom and I. And to my beloved son Johnny who is in heaven, I can't wait to see you again, my wonderful son. To my loving dog, "Disney".

A special thank you to Nel Penney, a great author in her own right, for her expert loving care in editing this book, and for all her hard work.

To my mother and father for teaching me to pray—I thank you from the bottom of my heart! I give thanks to my mother-in-law, Carol Horne; to my sisters-in-law, Sherri Sumstine and Arlene Joyner; to my brother Mike "Preacher Mike" who is in heaven. Thank you to my Brother Dewey, and to my sisters, Sharon and Judy.

Thank you to my Chief Intercessor, Elizabeth McDonald-Rodrigues.

I want to acknowledge and give special thanks to my faithful armor bearers: Senior Armor Bearer Edward Crespo, (you are the best friend and Armor Bearer in the world), Pastor Al

Flores, Raul Martinez, Eric Euren, and Mindy Flynn.

Thank you to all to the amazing pastors. Wishing I could mention all of your names here, but you know who you are; *you are the true inspiration of this book.*

Thank you to Dr. Dick & Dee Eastman, Brother Dick, my mentor, (who, in my opinion is the Father of the Prayer Movement), you have taught me so.....much!

Thank you to Dick Simmons; Mama Choi, mother-in-law of Dr. David Youngi Cho; Suzette Hattingh, Intercessor to Reinhart Bonke; Armin Gesswein, Intercessor to Billy Graham; Leonard Ravenhill; Helen Ko, Director of Prayer Mountain; Nancy Harmon: and to Eddie and Alice Smith, wow what a team! Eddie, thank you for your guidance, and wise counsel.

Thank you to dear friends: (Pastor Dennis McGuire, you have been there with me through thick and through thin— Thank you buddy), Bishop Sherwood Carthen, Pastor Joe Talancon, Arlene McElhenney, Shari Bonnard, Brother Barney Blackwell, Tom Salter, Tim Thrift, Shaun Gartman, Michelle Bryant, Felix Gonzales, Pastor Glen Cole, Elaine "Mom" Mercer, plus many more. You all know who you are.....!

A special thank you to our National Advisors of the United States National Prayer Council: Eddie & Alice Smith, Mark Gonzales, Nancy McDaniel, T.C. Kim, Pastor Wally Magdangal, Pastor "Sistah Pat" Rivers, Dr. Candi MacAlpine, and Scott Darling.

Finally, Reverend Samuel & Eva Rodriguez, thank you for the privilege to serve you and our amazing church family at New Season Christian Worship Center as your Pastor of Prayer. Pastor Samuel, I am humbled and honored to be your friend and Chief Intercessor My prayer is that I will be faithful to serve you well. **Let's change the world together!**

TABLE OF CONTENTS

Forward
by Dr. Dick Eastman

"Years ago I founded the Prayer Corps ministry in Sacramento, California, and Ted Rose was one of the key prayer leaders who kept the fires burning in the years that followed. I have a deep respect for Ted as an intercessor and a fellow mobilizer of prayer.

Ted's book *Pastors Need Prayer: Holding up Your Pastors' Arms through Prayer* is truly a message the Church must hear today. We often think of our pastors as intercessors for us, but we don't realize just how much our pastors need our prayers as well!

From my early years as a youth pastor at a Midwest church, when I had a handful of volunteer staff, to now when I have become responsible for the spiritual leadership of more than 4,000 supported staff members of Every Home for Christ (the evangelism ministry I direct). In addition, there are some 40,000 monthly volunteers in 120 nations, and I can personally attest to the unique challenges of a pastor's life— and their genuine need for prayer!

On the pages that follow, Ted sheds light on the practical and spiritual realities faced by our pastors on a day-to-day basis. He reveals the great need for prayer and spiritual support among the pastorate, and he helps us understand what meeting that need looks like. Ted offers useful guidance as we seek to become armor-bearers for the pastors in our lives, with valuable insights and biblical illustrations to guide us along the way.

Ted is a close friend of and intercessor for countless pastors (including myself!), and I know he has seen the fruit of prayer for those in leadership. Like Ted, I am a passionate advocate for the power of prayer. Imagine the impact of every local church praying passionately for its pastors! I believe this book, if we will follow Ted's urging, has the potential to truly transform our churches today. As we pray for our pastors, systematically and daily, we will see powerful churches led by wise and godly men and women, if we will unite behind them in fervent prayer."

Dr. Dick Eastman

International President

Every Home for Christ

President of America's National Prayer Committee

Special Message
by Reverend Samuel Rodriguez

"There's a fine line between the prophetic and the pathetic. Surrounded by a pathetic reality, full of relativism, decadence, apathy, and constant attempts by the enemy to silence the voices of righteousness, today's Pastors require the engagement of men and women anointed to intercede on their behalf. Pastor Ted Rose represents the quintessential intercessor. As a result of Rev. Rose and a lifetime committed to servant leadership via the conduit of praying for ministers, countless lives have been saved, pastors covered, and pulpits protected.

Personally, I can attest that as I travel in advancing the Lamb's agenda, I approach the podium with confidence knowing that Christ is my rock, and his servant, Ted Rose, stands in the gap so I can preach the word, in and out of season. This book is a must read for every Pastor, intercessor and servant committed to igniting a prayer canopy so that Pastors can shine the light of Christ in this generation."

Reverend Samuel Rodriguez

President

National Hispanic Christian Leadership Conference – (40,000 Churches)

Hispanic Evangelical Association

Introduction

Every day across our land, too many pastors submit their resignations after years of faithfulness and sacrifice. These pastors have left their churches exhausted, injured and heartbroken. If their family has survived, these pastors may go to the next assignment, or they may turn away from pastoring altogether-many feeling discouraged and disgraced.

It's my heart's deepest cry, and prayer that the Lord will use this book with its prayerful message to **open *your* eyes to the truth** of what is happening to our pastors. I have given my entire life to praying and mobilizing prayer for Pastors, all of these years. I have had an opportunity to preach/teach the message in this book to literally hundreds of congregations. We have over 200,000 belivers, now in over 100 countries, praying everyday for their Pastors.

Almost every believer says in his or her heart, "**Not my pastor,** it couldn't happen to him or her." But in my lifetime of prayer and counseling for hundreds of pastors during their pain and discouragement, let me tell you-it could happen—even to your pastor, as I've witnessed too many times to count.

Dear man and woman of God, allow the Lord to use you in prayer, before it is too late for your pastor to ensure that he doesn't end up as a statistic or a victim of ministry.

Whether you are a new or mature Christian, allow God to use your prayers to make the difference. All prayers are powerful and create change.

At the end of this book, you will find a prayer asking God to pass the mantle of prayer to you. The Lord will take you from where you are right now in your prayer life and launch you into a life-long school of prayer at the feet of Jesus.

If you take this biblical challenge to be a praying Christian, you will experience an unprecedented walk with the Lord in constant communion with Him. Watch His miracles take place on every hand. The early church was born through prayer, and prayer births miracles today as well.

Together on our knees we will change the world, bring in the harvest and fulfill the Great Commission—in our lifetime.

One thing that I want to make totally clear. As we respond to the call of prayer from the Lord Himself. **The ultimate goal of all prayer is to win the lost to Jesus Christ.** Praying for our pastors, leaders and everyone else will ultimately bring people to the Lord.

With respect and love to each of you, I thank you for reading this book. I pray it will be a blessing to you.

Chapter 1
Your Pastor is a Target

"...Strike the shepherd and the sheep... will be scattered"
(Matthew 26:31). NIV

Aren't you glad you have a pastor in your life? I met a gentleman from the Oakland Dream Center who heard about our prayer ministry for pastors. He shared a phrase he used regarding his pastor, and I thought it was very accurate and perceptive. It was *"Without my pastor, I'd have a disaster."* He must have experienced the great benefits of sharing with his pastor his burdens and prayer requests. Now, just because you have a pastor, that doesn't necessarily mean you won't have a disaster, but at least you know who to call when you have one. Do you know that your pastor needs help too sometimes? He needs prayer and God's intervention just like you do.

From the moment your pastor was called to ministry, he became a strategic target of the devil. **You cannot see it, but there is a bull's-eye target on your pastor.** The enemy is working 24 hours a day, 7 days a week, and 365 days a year to destroy your pastor and to render him or her ineffective.

Who does your pastor call when he needs help? Who stands with him, beside him, praying for his needs as he does for yours? Pastors are experiencing an unprecedented wave of attacks, stresses, challenges, obstacles and difficulties. They need our prayers as never before.

The best example of this is found in the life of Jesus Christ. The devil used King Herod, who issued a decree to kill all male children under the age of 2 in Bethlehem, just hoping to kill the infant Savior, baby Jesus. This was the devil's first, failed attempt to kill Jesus Christ. However, the devil is relentless and ruthless and will never give up. Early in Christ's ministry, after He was filled with the Holy Spirit, **He was led into the wilderness by the Spirit but was tempted by the devil as revealed in Matthew, Chapter 4.** The truth is that the devil had a bull's-eye target on Jesus but failed at his many attempts to lure Christ into temptation to render him useless to the Father.

The devil's goal was to prevent Jesus from accomplishing His mission, purpose, and destiny by destroying Him. The devil failed because Jesus faithfully and daily spent secluded, precious alone time with His Father in prayer and followed His Father's will in obedience, even when facing the most gruesome, painful death. He knew His death had a special purpose of victory for the Kingdom of God; it was to bless the world with forgiveness and restored relationships with His Father. Yet when Jesus Christ needed the prayers of his close disciples, they failed him. He asked for prayer partners in the most agonzing moments in His earthly life. He said to His disciples, **"My soul is exceedingly sorrowful, even unto death."Matthew 26:18 KJV**

The late great Pastor Adrian Rodgers, of Bellevue Baptist Church, in Memphis, Tennessee, (with over 29,000 members) once said, "The Bible says, in **Matthew 26:31 NIV, "If you strike the shepherd,... the sheep... will be**

scattered." *This is the devil's goal in action-to strike, wound, steal and destroy lives. It is disastrous destruction. This reveals one of the devil's goals; he has aimed all the artillery of hell at our pastors.*

You see the devil has limited resources, abilities, and time. And his time is running out. The Bible says, **"Therefore rejoice, ye heavens, and ye that dwell in them. Woe to the inhabiters of the earth and of the sea! for the devil is come down unto you, having great wrath, because he knoweth that he hath but a short time" (Revelation12:12).** KJV The devil roams about with great wrath seeking the most effective and destructive means to render pastors ineffective. His goal is to scatter the sheep, or the followers of Christ, by striking the leaders. That is why your pastor is more strategic to the devil than you. The enemy, aware of his short time frame, must focus the bulk of his forces against the most strategic target he can find, and that target is your pastor. The question is: **Will the enemy have to fight through your faithful prayers to do so?**

Pastor Dee Duke, of Jefferson Baptist Church in Jefferson City, Oregon, once said, *"The devil has big demons and little demons. He sends the big ones to pastors and their families, and he sends the little ones to everyone else."* This seasoned pastor, who is covered spiritually through the strong, effective prayers of his congregation, is speaking from many years of experience. His Church averages 16 prayer meetings each week. The devil knows that if he can cause your pastor to fall or fail, he can affect nearly everyone else in the congregation; but if he causes you to fall or fail, he will generally only impact a relative few.

Recently, I received a emergency phone call from a respected and dedicated pastor who said to me, **"Pastor Ted, I have a**

loaded gun with me right now, and I am ready to use it."
After thirty years of pastoring his church, he had reached a
crisis time in his life and felt so devastated that he actually
believed there was no other way out than to kill himself. I
listened to him, and prayed for him, and walked him through
several weeks of pain and trauma. His denomination did
nothing to minister to him, to his family, or to his church. He
felt alone, overburdened, and hopeless-with no one to turn to.
Many of our denominations do not have an atmosphere of
safety and forgiveness for hurting or damaged leaders.
Consequently, they have no place to go for help and support,
and no one to confide in about their true struggles and issues.
Leaders and members of many denominations are more
punitive and discipline-oriented rather than tender or loving.
They fail to extend the same understanding love of Christ to
their leaders, or pastors, that they would give to everyone
else. **Therefore, most pastors must privately carry their
burdens alone.** After living this way for so long, many
pastors eventually crack and become public stories of
disgrace; or worse, they even sometimes take their own life
by suicide.

Earlier this past year, a pastor of a mainline denomination
became so burned out and exhausted that he, in desperation,
took his own life. He left behind a heartbroken teenage son
and daughter, and a grieving wife. This news devastated the
entire city. He was not an uncaring pastor who did not have
his priorities right, but rather a family man, well respected in
the community, and a third generation minister.

What happened? If you were to ask his congregation if
anyone could ever imagine this outcome was possible, they
would have said, **"No way! Not our pastor."**

Having spent many years as a confidential mentor and

intercessor to pastors, I can tell you this can happen to anyone; and if you don't believe it, then you haven't seen today's current news. A month after the above pastor took his own life, another pastor, just an hour from our region, was found dead, hanging in his own barn. This pastor actually was a pastor to pastors who gathered believers together specifically to pray for pastors.

Why did this happen? Why is this happening all over our nation? Could it be for lack of prayer? The Bible makes it quite clear, **"…yet ye have not, because ye ask not" (James 4:2)**.KJV When are we going to wake up and start praying for our pastors? When are we going to pray for our pastor's needs, for direction, and for a greater faith? When are we going to pray for Jesus to guide our pastors with His wisdom in all their decisions? When are we going to pray that God will protect and provide for pastors, their marriages and families, and the church? When are we going to pray that pastors will jealously guard their private time alone with God? Pastors need your prayers desperately.

Our pastors need prayer for a safe environment of transparency and openness where they can share with other leaders their true, personal, heavy burdens and concerns? We forget that they face the same everyday issues and problems as their sheep.

Unfortunately, most pastors are elevated by their people as spiritual giants. They rarely can be seen as mere mortal human beings with everyday issues just like everyone else.

The enemy will attack your pastor with temptations and attempt to gain footholds in his character. The enemy will

31

also try to discourage your pastor, and pursue his family, or use sickness or disease. Destroying your pastor's effectiveness is one of Satan's greatest goals. The point is: the devil has an entire array of attacks to throw at your pastor that you can't even begin to imagine. Many times the enemy uses needy and hurting church members to build close relationships with your pastor for the express purpose of creating a discrediting situation that will ultimately end in the pastor's injured reputation and integrity.

It is rare indeed for a pastor not to experience a devastating betrayal by a close associate; a friend who pledges lifelong loyalty and friendship, yet becomes the one who turns on him and leads a revolt against him. This betrayal produces scars and personal disappointments that can add up over many years, and can cause a pastor to live a guarded and alienated existence. The pastor may never know who is genuine or who is jockeying for position, and one day, be the one to thrust in the personal dagger at close range.

Usually, when I share openly what is truly going on in the lives of pastors, people say they had no idea this was occurring. One of the main reasons for this book, *Pastors Need Prayer*, is to take the veil off people's eyes to reveal these disturbing facts, and to seek your urgent prayers. **However, we will never get serious about prayer until we see pastors' true and desperate needs, that the enemy attacks pastors fiercely, and realize prayer's effectiveness.**

Jesus reveals the enemy's purpose contrasted to His, **"The thief cometh not, but for to steal, and to kill, and to destroy: I am come that they might have life, and that they might have it more abundantly" (John 10:10).KJV**

You and I can severely hinder and damage the enemy's

attacks through prayer and our prayers will produce the abundant life both in ourselves and our pastors. Would you commit to pray for your pastor and family, and daily praise God for them?

Every church would do well to develop a mindset and action plan to care for their pastor. This plan would contribute to the prosperous growth of the church and to individual members as well. A group of respected leaders could: select a devoted prayer team who continually studies the Scriptures and constantly covers pastor, his or her family, and the church in fervent prayer; choose a confidential select few to listen to and pray with and for pastor's individual, confidential burdens with compassion, concern and direction rather than judgment; ensure the pastor takes adequate leave time; ensure the pastor is blessed well financially; ensure the pastor is provided ample time to pursue personal needs and life goals; ensure the pastor is provided with health and retirement blessings; and overall, is treated well with respect and love by all church members.

Is there such a committee in your church to oversee the personal welfare of your pastor and his family? It would be the greatest blessing for your church, and for every church, to develop this committee.

I have seen that so many churches are more focused on what their pastor can do for them rather than what they can do for their pastor for lack of knowledge and understanding. Many members elevate pastors to superhuman status, failing to realize pastors are human with real challenges and needs that can only be met through much fervent prayer, your prayer.

Confess your faults one to another, and pray one for another, that ye may be healed. The effectual fervent

prayer of a righteous man availeth much (James 5:16). KJV

Ted Rose

Chapter 2
The Crisis in the Ministry

"Obey them that have the rule over you and submit yourselves: for they watch for your souls, as they that must give an account, that they may do it with joy, and not with grief: for that is unprofitable for you." (Hebrews 13:17). KJV

As promised in Chapter 1, I'm listing the stunning and eye-opening statistics of many pastors' plights throughout our nation. These dismal statistics are accurate and certainly not pleasing or edifying, but we must face the truth of the current crisis surrounding our beloved pastors in order to be transformed and used to further God's kingdom. As you read the below facts, please remember that there are many pastors who are some of the most special men and women of God that have ever walked the planet. Their love, sacrifice, and servants' heart are what makes them such great gifts of God to all of us. However, many are under attack from many directions and this is why we have the below statistics. Please read them with prayerful hearts.

What does a ministry crisis look like?
Recent studies provide the troubling state of the life of the

pastor.

➤ **1,500** pastors leave the ministry each month due to moral failure, spiritual burnout, or contention in their churches.

➤ **50%** of pastors are so discouraged and say they would leave the ministry if they could, but don't feel they have the skills to earn a living another way.

➤ **70%** of pastors fight chronic depression that never leaves.

➤ **40%** of pastors shared they've had an extramarital affair since they entered the ministry.

➤ **70%** of pastors don't have a close friend, confidant or mentor.

➤ **95%** of pastors don't pray regularly with their spouses.

➤ **80%** of pastors shared they spend less than 15 minutes a day in prayer.

➤ **70%** of pastors revealed the only time they spend in the Word of God, or the Bible, is when they are preparing their sermons.

➤ **Over 50%** of pastors reported they viewed internet pornography last year.

➤ **80%** of pastors' adult children surveyed have had to seek professional help for depression.

➤ **The majority** of pastors' wives surveyed shared the most destructive event in their marriage or family was the day they entered the ministry.

➤ **50%** of pastors' marriages are ending in divorce.

➤ **80%** of pastors' spouses wish their spouse would choose another profession.

➤ **4,000 churches open** each year, but over **7,000 churches close.** We have lost over 33,000 churches more than we have gained in the last ten years.

These ominous, heartbreaking facts reveal the continuing crisis in ministry.

Let's clarify the definition of "crisis":

Webster defines the word "crisis" as:

> *"The turning point for better or worse, distress or disordered function, a decisive moment, an unstable or crucial state of affairs in which a decisive change is impending, especially one with the distinct possibility of a highly undesirable outcome, a situation which has reached a critical phase, a boiling point, breaking point, emergency, crossroads, crunch time, flash point, head, and Zero Hour.*

This definition describes the accurate state of our pastors and their families, and churches. If we listen, we will hear their cries for a godly, loving response.

Did you know that every weekend over fifty per cent of pastors in the pulpits of our nation don't even want to be there? They feel trapped.

They've spent years studying the Bible and completing Bible

College or Seminary. They had a purpose of ministry, but in a relatively short time discover that they are burned out and discouraged with no vision or hope of a future plan.

A pastor's great expertise is, gained through the completion of Bible College or Seminary. It's to worship, pray, and proclaim God's truth of Jesus Christ through total dependence upon the Holy Spirit's clear message of repentance, revelation and truth. There is an expectation and trust in God to penetrate hardened hearts for total transformation of themselves and their church.

A pastor's hope is to effectively share God's Word of Truth to transform their church family, and to make bold, effective disciples of Jesus who are willing to take the Good News to the ends of the earth and to show God's love in good works.

Here is an example: Many years ago as I was preparing to teach a citywide, Change the World School of Prayer Seminar for Every Home for Christ. I spent several months flying each weekend to preach in many churches that were sponsoring this citywide event. I had the honor to spend time alone with each pastor and became heartbroken as I listened to their pain and burdens. I encountered far too many pastors who were struggling in their daily lives and ministries. They couldn't share their problems with anyone in the church. They had no one to confide in .Why?

Because everyone expected them to be perfect and strong at all times. These pastors felt vulnerable and unable to confide in their denominational leaders, as these confidences could possibly result in disciplinary action or removal or judgment. They wouldn't dare seek other pastors in town because they feared possible betrayal of this personal information used against them—to gain advantage in their city. They felt trapped and isolated. This completely broke my heart wide open to seek the face of God to make a difference. I pleaded with the Lord to use me to help pastors in their most crucial moment of their lives. This book is a product of those desperate prayers.

Pastors' families suffer as a result. Personally, I have found few benefits of being a pastor's child. In fact, pastors' lives can be filled with much heartache, which will affect the lives of their children.

The statistics reveal that eight out of ten pastors' children will end up seeking professional psychiatric help for depression. Why is this so?

I will share from my experience: My parents were in ministry for over fifty years, so I experienced life as a pastor's child. It was filled with challenges that most people rarely imagine or experience. The congregation scrutinized my life. They examined everything from my words and actions, to choices of clothing, to choices of music, to choices of friends, to choices of movies, and on and on. You get the idea.

Life was lived and clearly revealed in what ministry refers to as the **"Fish Bowl."** It's no wonder that so many youth end up jaded, rebellious, and damaged.

Imagine the chaos, confusion, and disillusionment created in the young heart as your dad, your family, and you endure criticism, ridicule, and judgment, all inherent in the attacks of your closest associates, and all in the name of God. It's difficult to assimilate and understand.

The divorce rate of pastors is staggering. Far too many

divorce and feel its destruction and disgrace and may even turn to suicide. It is tragic.

From personal experience, I understand that pastors need help, encouragement, and prayer. So, I have reached out to many pastors who now call me on a daily basis to share their struggles, to unload their pain, and to request prayer.

Pastors face difficult and tragic circumstances. To support them with their innermost heartaches and needs, I began a ministry as a personal and confidential intercessor. For most of these godly leaders, I became the only person on earth who they felt comfortable enough with to share their hearts and innermost secrets, without fear and without judgment. In this safe realm, together we seek God's face and His counsel, His wisdom and guidance in prayer, and trust God to reveal His plan.

Sadly, far too many pastors haven't been discipled or shown how to have an effective prayer life. Prayer and its importance are rarely taught in our Bible colleges or seminaries. And many of our pastors have never seen their own pastors as godly examples of prayer.

Life without prayer means defeat is near. Without prayer we become weak and defenseless, and we quickly fall prey to the enemy's lies, to his subtle deceit, and to his destruction. Consider Satan's goal to lie, to steal, and destroy God's creation. The enemy wants to scatter the sheep, isolate them, and render them hopeless and helpless. Currently, it appears that much of our professional pastorate ministry lacks prayer.

We've seen Satan working from generation to generation, to systematically remove prayer from our nation, schools, churches, families, and even the pastorate. Churches, pastors and families not bathed in prayer result in powerless and destroyed ministries that are wracked with disgrace while the sheep are scattered.

Why is this happening? It's because God no longer has first place or priority in our hearts and lives. We've lost our passionate love for God, our commitment to His will, and consequently have lost the victorious power of God that comes through seeking God's face in prayer.

But Jesus showed us a better way. He showed us the powerful results of prayer. Jesus prayed much and showed that with prayer, faith, belief, and commitment to obey God that all could be blessed. Jesus even told us to **always pray and never give up (See Luke 18:1).**

The crisis in the ministry is clear----**WE'RE NOT PRAYING!!!!. Are you** praying for the pastor's wisdom, guidance, and needs? We see the visible results and statistics of tragic consequences when Christians aren't devoting themselves to prayer for their pastors or listening to and following God's lead. We've seen pastors fall in this realm as well.

I am thinking of a particular denomination that statistically devotes more time to prayer on average than any other denomination. **They average just one minute and forty-five seconds of prayer for a two-hour church service.** This includes the opening prayer, offering prayer and the closing prayer. Someone has stolen corporate prayer from our churches knowing that this is the most powerful prayer there is. It was corporate prayer that gave birth to the church.

WE ARE ALL CALLED TO PRAY

The Bible teaches all of us to pray without ceasing. **"Rejoice**

always, pray without ceasing, in everything give thanks; for this is the will of God in Christ Jesus for you" (1 Thessalonians 5:16-18). NKJV

Praying without ceasing doesn't mean to ignore daily responsibilities, but to always be connected to our Heavenly Father in an attitude of prayer, consulting and communing with Him first in all our ways. It means we follow in Jesus' obedient footsteps and trust God. It's a daily choice and sacrifice to lay down our own agendas in order to seek God's face and His will. **How much time do you spend in prayer each day?**

Prayer is more than a powerful channel of communication from man to God and God to man. It's a vibrant lifeline strengthened with wisdom and hope that illuminates a new direction for those seeking God's face. It is a revelation of total transformation and cleansing.

God transforms our hearts' greatest desires to conform to His greatest desires—or His will. As we stay connected to Him in prayer, He does the work within. Our transformation is found in seeking His face. This transformation, brought about by prayer, is sufficient grace and provision for the ministry in crisis, for pastors, for our churches, and for our families.

When your pastor first answered the call to become a pastor, he began his journey with a great love for the Lord. He lived in the Word of God and constantly searched the scriptures seeking to know God better. He gave himself to the Lord for the work of the ministry. His only desire was to love and please the Lord.

As time, experiences, and trials permeated your exuberant pastor's life, he discovered his great desire for the Lord and

His Word had faded. The pastor wasn't filled with desire to open God's Word. Many times he wouldn't open the Bible that he once loved—except to prepare for his weekly-required sermons. How did this happen?

There are many reasons why this happens. Perhaps one of the reasons is that we fail to consult God first. **We fail to pray first,** and we fail to listen to God. We fail to obey His will, and we choose our own way instead. We lose our first love, our passion for God. We fail to put Him first in everything. This always leads to disastrous consequences. **For lack of prayer and not putting God first, we fall and we fail.**

As statistics reveal, there are many pastors, perhaps more than forty percent, who have made the great mistake of committing adultery. Yes, some pastors are committing adultery. As a result, they live with consequences of incredible guilt, with no one to talk to about their secret, and no place to go for help.

Meanwhile they hope and pray that no one ever discovers their darkest secrets. They feel ineffective and hypocritical standing in front of their congregation preaching the Word of God week after week, while cowering inside with the heavy burden of mind-paralyzing guilt and fear.

Far too often the ministry is seriously compromised, in tragic crisis, and has become crippled, disgraced and defeated as you can see. Is there hope of a transformation for our pastors and for our churches? If so, what would that be?

Pastors Need Prayer

Chapter 3
"The Answer to the Crisis"

"Now I beseech you, brethren, for the Lord Jesus Christ's sake, and for the love of the Spirit, that ye strive together with me in your prayers to God for me" (Romans 15:30). KJV

Yes, there is an answer, and a hope of transformation. **You can be a huge part of the answer to this crisis.** Your faithful, persistent, and fervent prayers will make all the difference in this world. You can uphold your pastor in prayer.

Let me ask you a crucial question: **If not you, then who? Who else is going to pray for your pastor?**

Can someone please tell me where I can go, who I can talk to, and how I can find the willing soul who will lift up your pastor before the throne of God in prayer?

Who will stand with your pastor when he makes a mistake? Who will look out for his welfare and lift him up when he is down? Who will encourage your pastor while others are throwing stones? Who will offer words of affirmation instead of criticism? Who will remain faithful even while others are bolting for a more thriving church or seeking a more charismatic leader? Who will weep with your pastor when he weeps, when the struggle gets hard and lonesome? Are you the one your pastor can count on, to intercede for him before God? **If not you, then who?**

The most powerful example of the need to pray for your Pastor or leader is found in the example of Jesus Christ and his disciples. This is where, on night of Jesus' betrayal by Judas, we find the Lord taking His disciples to the garden for prayer and then asking His 3 closest companions to come and pray with him through the night. Then as the Lord anguished in prayer, he found his disciples asleep. He didn't ignore their failure but woke them up. **Is He waking you up right now from your slumber when it comes to prayer?** He woke them up and asked them a very important question. "Can you not come and pray with me for even one hour?" Then he returned to prayer, only to pray so intensely that he began to sweat drops of blood. Medical experts will attest that when the body is under such pressure, the sweat glands of a human body will excrete drops of blood. This was an incredible scene that the disciples were witnessing. And yet they fell asleep again. This time the Lord woke them up again and said **"My soul is exceedingly sorrowful even to the point of death."Matthew 26:18 KJV** He was crying out-Please pray with me, I need you right now more than I have ever needed you ever before. Did you know that your pastor has reached these same moments in their ministry? **During the dark night of his soul, who could he call within his congregation to stay awake with him?** You got it- they fell asleep again. The Lord then repeated Himself. **Can you not spend one hour with me in prayer?** They fell asleep again. Then Jesus gave us insight into the cause of this failure. He said,**"the spirit indeed is willing, but the flesh is weak."** **Matthew 26:41 KJV** Both the disciples and Jesus were tired but what was the difference? Jesus had developed the daily habit of prayer, and had control or mastery over his flesh. Rather than letting his flesh determine whether he would pray through the night or sleep, he chose to pray.

Dick Eastman, President of Every Home for Christ, **a worldwide ministry that has seen over 128 million decisions for Christ since 1953** states, *"When people cease to pray, whatever the reasons, Christians backslide, youth rebel, preachers leave pulpits, mission fields close, and denominations die."*

One of the most powerful examples in modern history of an intercessor praying for a Christian leader is the story of Billy Graham's intercessor and prayer leader, Armin Gesswein. Armin was a pastor himself . In 1948 he invited young Billy Graham to Los Angeles to hold a crusade. When the unknown Graham arrived, Armin formed a prayer movement and when Billy Graham preached in the now famous Tent, **Armin Gesswein led 1,000 men in prayer in a tent next to the tent where Billy was preaching.** This launched the wonderful ministry of one of the greatest Evangelists in America's history. No man, including your pastor, can accomplish their mission unless there is enough prayer to back it up and to support it.

The Apostle Paul asked for prayer from his fellow believers as well as from his new converts more than any other church leader in the Bible. Is there any wonder that his ministry was so effective, and that the Lord used him to pen two-thirds of the New Testament!

The prayers of the Church propelled his ministry. Paul prayed as well, and he also made the right choices to obey God's will, not his own will, even if it meant his own life—which eventually it did.

Paul stirred up the church for the love of Jesus and asked for prayers to uphold him and his ministry. Paul was filled with the Holy Spirit to accomplish a huge mission. Paul was on fire for Jesus and wholeheartedly dedicated to Him. Passion illuminated Paul's soul for the Lord as his first love. Paul was steadfast in faithfulness and commitment to Jesus until death. Paul's desire was to do and finish God's plan and work for his life. Jesus transformed him, and he walked in a perpetual relationship with Him. Paul knew he needed the many prayers of believers and asked for them.

The great revivalist R.A. Torrey said, *"Any church may have a mighty man of God for it's pastor, if it's willing to pay the price, and that price is not a big salary, but great praying. It's up to you."*

I would like to ask again, if not you then who?

Without your prayers we will remain in crisis. But through our prayers together, we can accomplish great things.

Apostle Paul stated, **"Now I beseech you, brethren, for the Lord Jesus Christ's sake, and for the love of the Spirit, that ye strive together with me in your prayers to God for me" (Romans 15:30) KJV**

One translation says it another way, **"I beg you to pray for me" World English Translation.**

Paul is literally begging the church to pray for him. Why?

It is because Paul encountered the powerful and living God. Paul knew there was great power found in prayer. Paul's life and mission were facing great risks. His life and mission were under fire and assault from the devil. Paul knew that the only way he would be able to carry out his ministry would be to have continual, persistent, and effectual prayer undergirding everything that he did.

Why do we allow ourselves to be so arrogant to think that we could accomplish our mission and destiny in life without prayer when the Son of God, Jesus Christ, lived his entire life and ministry dependent upon prayer? Isn't that called pride? Isn't it the same pride that caused Satan to fall? Wasn't Jesus giving us an example to follow Him in prayer as well so we won't fall?

Armin Gesswein, the late great intercessor for Reverend Billy Graham said, *"Make no mistake, when the Lord builds a church, He builds a prayer meeting."*

The early church was conceived and birthed in an upper room of prayer. **For ten days, over one hundred twenty faithful followers of Christ prayed** until heaven came down to earth and an outpouring of the promised Holy Spirit rushed in such a powerful way that it spread throughout their known world in a relatively short period of time, and soon—to the ends of the earth. The outpouring of the Holy Spirit is still prospering over two thousand years later   because we are speaking God's truth.

Dick Eastman, said in his book, *No Easy Road*, *"The early church was born out of a call to prayer by no less than Jesus Christ himself, and was sustained in its formative years by obedience to that call."*

There is a flaw in our western culture of independence and individualism that puts the pastor on an

unsustainable pedestal. This leads to great pressure on pastors to always be the spiritual giant in the room.

Throughout years of prayer ministry, I have found this one thing to be true—most pastors will not ask their people to pray for them. So I am asking us to make prayer for our pastor a priority. **By doing this, we can become part of the solution of this ministry crisis.**

Honestly, I think that most pastors are embarrassed to ask their congregation to pray for them. Perhaps church members feel that they pay their pastors to do the ministry; therefore, pastors should be praying for them, the flock, rather than the other way around.

The goal of revealing the inner circle circumstances that many of our precious pastors' are facing is to encourage you to be a part of the solution to this crisis. There are many ways to become the solution to this crisis in ministry.

One solution would be to form a dedicated Pastor's Committee. The committee's sole purpose and mission would be to look out for the well-being and care of the pastor and his or her family.

I am not referring to a scrutinizing, ecclesiastical oversight committee that constantly inflicts unrealistic pressure on the pastor to perform, but a group of loving, humble, and caring servants of Jesus who pray for their pastor.

This group could show God's love by lovingly and regularly communicate with their pastor to determine any of his needs and to discuss how he and family are doing spiritually, physically, mentally, and emotionally. A relationship of trust, understanding, and love could be built where the pastor would feel safe and comfortable to share his heart in any of these areas without fear of retribution for himself or family members.

Here is an example of the official job description and duties for this group:

> ➢ **Ensure** that everyone in this group commits to daily prayer for pastor.

> ➢ **Ensure** that your pastor has appropriate days off each week.

> ➢ **Ensure** that your pastor has ample vacation time allocated.

> ➢ **Ensure** that there is a personal growth budget for your pastor to attend retreats, seminars, and conferences.

> ➢ **Ensure** that there is a healthy and non-combative relationship with the Elders Board and deacons and pastor.

> ➢ **Ensure** there is a zero tolerance for gossip about the pastor and his family at all times, especially those family members in leadership.

> ➢ **Ensure** that all of the work of the church, doesn't fall upon just the pastor.

As discussed before, saints can be a solution to this crisis by praying for pastors. We can pray daily for all the areas that are listed in the revealed statistics and more. You, your family, your church, and your pastor will all be blessed as a result of a sincere prayer like this one:

Pastors Need Prayer

Here is an example prayer for your pastor that you can pray.

Father God, I am thinking of my pastor today and ask You to please transform my pastor's heart and make his heart's desire You. Strengthen my pastor to stand strong against temptation and deliver him from temptation by taking the Sword of the Spirit, which is the Word of God and speak it **with authority.** Empower my pastor to pick up the Shield of Faith to quench all the fiery darts of the evil one, and wear the Belt of Truth, and the Shoes of Peace. Remind him that he is secure with You while wearing the Breastplate of Righteousness and the Helmet of Salvation.

Lord, please equip my pastor with Your Truth that delights his soul. Give him quality time to spend daily in Your Presence for his refreshment and wisdom and guidance.

Lord, please lead my pastor to organize and prioritize his daily tasks so You are first in everything. Please lead my pastor to spend time soaking up Your Word as a sponge, highlighted in prayer with You. Reveal to him how to be successful and prosperous by obeying You. Please heal him physically and spiritually, mend his heart, and mend his family and loved ones. Give him ears to hear You and a desire to please You more than anything else in this world.

Father God, cause my pastor to grow in Your truth as he meditates on You and Your Word. Create in my pastor's heart a fervent passion for You and the things of Your kingdom instead of the world's treasures and pleasures. Father, please lead my pastor away from the subtle deceit and lust of this world. Please deliver him from these temporary pleasures that appear so beautiful but bring swift heartache and are gone by loss, destruction, or death. Help my pastor to store up treasures in heaven for him and his family.

Father, send encouragement to my pastor today in Your marvelous, loving way. Send wave after wave of refreshing. When the enemy tries to attack my pastor I ask you to thwart the attack and bring peace and protection. Remind my pastor that his joy is found in You, and that Your joy is his strength. Enable my pastor to remain connected to You at all times through an attitude of prayer, through always yielding to the whisper of Your Holy Spirit, and through quickly obeying Your will, not his own. Remind my pastor to treat others with respect, kindness, and godly love; to be that light that leads others to You. Even when others are unkind, insincere and hurtful, remind him to remember what You have said about him, rather than what others or the enemy says about him.

Father God, please supply all my pastor's needs and heart's desires as he seeks Your face. Remind my pastor to bring all his thoughts captive to You first before he continues with those thoughts into a plan of action. Remind my pastor to pray first about everything; pray on his thoughts before he makes plans, pray before he acts or speaks, and to give all his thoughts, words, plans and actions to you to transform, because You know his heart's thoughts and desires. Please align my pastor's thoughts and desires to Your thoughts and desires, Father God. Please assure my pastor of Your great love for him, that You love him more than he can imagine. Please assure him You also love his family and church. Please cause him to know that You want to bless him more than he can imagine with Your abundance here on earth and in heaven.

Dear God, please keep my pastor's heart pure and free of the lust of this world by keeping his eyes on Your beautiful face. Cause my pastor to meditate on the depth of Your love that You have for him which you showed by sacrificing Your life to give him everlasting life, and a beautiful and safe home in heaven one day.

Dear Father, fill my pastor with overwhelming love for You. Please give him fresh revelation of Your rich love that flows to his family, his wife, his church, and all those he comes into contact with. Please bless my pastor with true friends with whom to share burdens and joys and who will help him in times of need. Teach my pastor to cast his cares on You, and trust You. Remind him that You do not want him to worry; worry won't accomplish anything good for him or for Your kingdom. Show my pastor how to pray. God, please remind my pastor to remain thankful in everything.

Dear God, please lead my pastor and his wife and family to pray together every day. Lead my pastor to be a light that brightens his loved ones' days, and the light that leads others to You. Please bless my pastor and his family with Your treasures and with peace, unity, and comfort. Lord, please cause my actions to shout love to them all. Lord, please let me not judge my pastor or anyone until I first see I am perfect- I do not have any sin in my life. Lord, instead of judging, please show me what to do to help, show me how to show grace and mercy instead of judgment.

Dear Jesus, I praise Your holy name that I can come to the foot of Your cross and breathe in Your goodness and exhale my burdens. I praise You because You are an amazing and mighty God who loves me, and my pastor. You deserve all my praise and worship. Thank You for hearing and answering my prayers.

Lord, please bless all the saints in the true Church, those who belong to You by faith in Jesus' blood sacrifice alone. Enlighten us and unite us in Your love, peace, and joy and in

Your Will for our lives. Show us how to always be about Your business of showing love to the world and bringing all we can into Your kingdom to enjoy a safe, secure home with You one day throughout eternity, in Jesus name, **Amen.**

Your prayers don't have to be that long, just heartfelt and supportive in covering your pastor. He needs you and your prayers more than you will ever know.

These are a couple of ways to begin a transformation for our pastors, their families, and our churches. This will benefit the church and bless the saints as well. Can you think of other ways to bring beneficial change?

Remember, many of our pastors will leave the ministry wounded and ahead of their time if there is not an outpouring of your prayers within a peaceful and loving environment to uphold, sustain, and transform them and the church.

Here is a poem that the Lord gave to me, that asks the question: Who will hear the voice of the Lord calling them to be a praying Christian and also a believer who will pray for their Pastor and leadership?

"Who Will Pray For Your Pastor"

Poem by Ted Rose

Who is the one
Who will pray for their Pastor

Who is the one
Whose prayer will avert Satan's disaster

Pastors Need Prayer

Who is the one

Who will get down on their knees

Who is the one

Who will pray for their Pastor's needs

In prayer you make the difference as did Aaron and Hur
Because prayer hits its mark and changes how things were

Say yes to the call to give all and to lift
The arms of your pastor who, to you, is God's loving gift

You are the one whom God calls to care

You are the one to support your pastor in prayer

If you will pray, you can make a huge difference in the life and ministry of your pastor, church, and world!

Chapter 4
Your Pastor Is a Gift from God

"And I will give you pastors according to mine heart, which shall feed you with knowledge and understanding" (Jeremiah 3:15). KJV

If you have another version of the Bible other than King James, your Bible may use the word "shepherds" instead of "pastors" in the above Scripture. "These two words, "shepherds" and "pastors" are derived from the same Greek word "poimen," and are used interchangeably because they have the same definition.

People ask me, **"Why do I love pastors so much?"** It's because God loves pastors. I continue to love them even though they have hurt me, abused me, and taken advantage of me. Jesus said, **" Bless those who curse you and pray for those who mistreat you." See Luke 6:28. NIV** Jesus also commanded us **to love our enemies and pray for them. See Matthew 5:44.** In obedience, I choose to follow Jesus.

While I have had painful experiences with pastors, I have also served with some of the greatest men and women who faithfully serve as pastors. We are blessed by many who serve with sacrificial dedication as they lay down their lives for their flock.

If you are one of the wounded, who have been hurt by a pastor, please forgive him and continue on your journey with God. Don't carry the hurt of the past. **I would like to recommend a great book by R.T. Kendall, called Total Forgiveness. It is a classic and it is a life changer.** Remember, your pastor is human just like you and makes mistakes as well. Offer the same forgiving love God gave to both you and the world when Jesus died on the cross for us even though we were still sinning and far away from His Holiness. Forgiveness is God's love in action. Obeying God's commands always brings blessings. Forgiveness brings blessings of peace and healing to you and those around you.

Praise God for His great gifts! We serve an amazing God who loves us more than we can comprehend and more than words can express. God gives His children amazing gifts, and one of those amazing gifts is your pastor.

Pastors are highly valued by God and given to you according to His heart. God is the one who chose your pastor especially for you. Your pastor was selected, prepared, and anointed with your needs in mind to shepherd you with God's love, grace, and truth. Would you give thanks and praises to God right now for His gift of your pastor who watches over your soul?

If God has called your pastor to the ministry, then God alone has given him authority, and he answers directly to God. Your pastor's authority mirrors a servant's role—serving his own Master. Your pastor is not a king, a lord, or a dictator, but a humble servant to God. Your pastor has received a God-given role as your spiritual ruler, leader, and overseer; he's your shepherd. His relationship with you and others in the church is profound. The shepherd is actually one of the sheep. The pastor and church family all look to Jesus, our Master and Good Shepherd.

Perhaps you are wondering why there is a strong emphasis on the role of the pastor in this book. It's not my intent to elevate your pastor above the flock, or put him on a pedestal, but rather to present scripture to guide you in obedience to cherish and honor him. **Your pastor needs you—your support, encouragement, and continual prayers**.

Jesus Christ is the only one elevated onto His beautiful throne, above the flock, for He is our Good Shepherd who guides us all. Jesus is the Head of the church. It's His Body and He has all authority over the church.

God uses pastors to build up His church, and to protect and tend the flock. Pastors have great responsibilities. They must be faithful, above reproach, and committed to teach others the gospel of Christ through the Holy Spirit's guidance. Some of your pastor's duties are to oversee the church, rule over the church, feed the church, and guard the doctrine of the church against false teachings.

Your pastor works hard to feed the flock the truth of God's Word, to lead by example, and to protect the integrity of the gospel. Pastors rule over the church, but they must do it as diligent caretakers, and humble servants of God. A pastor's teachings should equip the saints for ministry to spread the good news of Jesus Christ and His love to save the lost. Your pastor is to be an example of faithfulness, truth, love, mercy, grace, diligence, self-control, and godliness, and he is answerable to God for his own leadership.

The Word of God shares some ways you can honor your

faithful, hard-working pastor so we all prosper. The Apostle Paul taught in **Galatians 6:6 that those who receive instruction in the Word should share all good things with their instructor.** Paul encourages believers to honor the elders who direct the affairs of the church well. He said they are worthy of **double honor**, especially those whose work is preaching and teaching. **"Let the elders that rule well be counted worthy of double honor, especially they who labor in the word and doctrine." (1 Timothy 5:17) NKJV**

What are some ways you can support, appreciate, and cherish your pastor with double honor? First, you can change your ways. It's so easy to let criticism slip through the lips. Therefore, prayerfully set your mind to offer encouragement instead of criticism. Tell your pastor how much his message means to you. Call him with encouraging words. You can support your pastor emotionally by planning special events occasionally for something he has done. Consider a special surprise now and then. Don't you like a little token of appreciation? Surprise him with a special lunch, dinner, or dessert every now and then, or a gift card for his favorite restaurant or coffee shop. Invite your pastor and family over for dinner. Also, strive to ensure your pastor has enough financial support for him and his family. Pastors are deserving of your good attention and appreciation.

Your pastor is a worker and teacher of God's Truth and is deserving of good wages as stated in **Luke 10:7. God loves a cheerful giver,** and when you give cheerfully, generously, and gratefully you are giving double honor to the faithful pastor who ministers to you.

If you realize you have fallen short in any of these or other areas God brings to mind, remember we serve a mighty God of mercy and grace. Simply confess these shortcomings to your loving, heavenly Father and ask for forgiveness and for a willing heart to change.

Perhaps you developed a critical attitude. It may have spilled over into insensitive, unkind words spewed at your pastor. Perhaps he was the target of harmful gossip, and you were a participant. Maybe you neglected to appreciate something he did, or failed to support him emotionally or financially. If so, simply ask God's forgiveness and guidance to show you how to honor your pastor. You can repent right now, which means to turn around and go in a different direction; do things differently. Become that solid rock of support that shows love and support for your pastor. Many years ago we had a special term for those who were the example of faithful servants of God. They were called, **"Pillars in the House of God"**. They would epitomize faithfulness, stability and support to leadership. We need this type of believers in the church family again. Tell others of this great responsibility to cherish and honor their pastor. You can grow a great support system by sharing these and other ideas with friends.

One day everyone will give an account of what they did with the gifts God has given them. Pray for wisdom, and trust in the Holy Spirit to reveal how to treat your pastor so that, on that day, you will be able to give a great report. Pray for your pastor, his family, and his ministry. Your pastor needs your faithful and powerful prayers for godly wisdom to effectively shepherd you as God intends so that, on that day, he will be able to give a great report to God as well.

What else can you do to give double honor to your pastor?

The Bible states: **"Have confidence in your leaders and submit to their authority, because they keep watch over you as those who must give an account. Do this so that**

their work will be a joy, not a burden, for that would be of no benefit to you" (Hebrews 13:17). NIV

At the Judgment Seat of Christ, each church member will individually give an account to the Lord of all they did and said. Each pastor will also give account as well. How terrible will it be to admit you criticized your pastor, the one God specifically chose, gifted, and anointed to shepherd you. How will you explain your arrogant attitude in refusing to submit to your pastor's God-given authority? **Bringing a God-ordained pastor grief for any reason will be unprofitable at the Judgment Seat of Christ. Instead, plan for your eternity right now by sowing seeds of loving obedience in prayer for your pastor so that both of you will reap the harvest of the Great Commission to the glory of God.**

Please hear and respond to this urgent and heartfelt cry, the core message of this book—your pastor needs much prayer, as he is responsible for keeping watch over many souls. Your pastor and church prosper when you pray. Pray for blessings to surround your pastor and his family. Pray for your pastor's leadership. Pray for your pastor to be effective and focused on preaching and teaching the truth of the gospel of Christ. Pray for God to plow up hardened hearts to receive the truth so the lost will be saved. So much will be accomplished with prayer.

Be humble with a teachable spirit. Don't allow pride to creep in and persuade you against your pastor's lead if he's teaching according to the Word of God.

Jesus referred to His followers as sheep in need of a shepherd for they could easily get lost, stolen, or killed. We are all children of the Most High God, and all of us, including your pastor, must always be mindful that our one true Head and

Ted Rose

Shepherd is not an earthly pastor,but the Lord Jesus Christ.

However, for a moment, reflect on the life of a pastor. Take time to consider the numerous responsibilities he must manage in overseeing the souls of many people. Can you imagine the intense pressure that could invade your pastor's peace? His decisions can affect many lives for years to come.

Your pastor is blessed by your tender loving care, your thoughtfulness, and prayers. Your prayers enable him to hear from God, and walk in God's divine wisdom. These blessings could weed out complaints and strife within the church. Please ask the Holy Spirit to continually fill your pastor to overflowing with wisdom, knowledge, understanding, and discernment to shepherd you with the love and care of God. Please pray for your pastor to yield and submit to the Holy Spirit's prompting to stand strong against temptation and sin, as you pray the same prayer for yourself.

The puppy story:
I would like to share an illustration that can give you a new perspective and outlook on taking care of your pastor. Remember a time when you saw precious little children near the entrance of a grocery store? They had something special to give away. You witnessed the children using their sweetest, child-like voices while holding the cutest, little puppies in their hands. "They're free," was their cry. **"Would you like a free puppy?"** They hoped to find their furry friends a good home. And you were the one who couldn't resist.

What if you took that puppy home with you, and when you got home you did everything you could to love your newly adopted puppy. You fed it good and pet it everyday. You spent time with your puppy and told your puppy that he/she

63

was the best puppy in the entire world. What would happen is that your puppy would grow to become a loving and caring animal and loyal member of your family, giving years of love back to you.

But suppose someone willingly took a free pet home only to abuse it. The puppy wasn't given much food, attention, or love. The puppy was kicked and scolded as if he was a bad puppy and was never touched in a loving way. If it survived the abuse, the puppy would grow and develop into a damaged dog for lack of tender loving care. The puppy would lack energy and trust, and he would cease to thrive.

Now, take a moment to visualize your pastor as if he was right there with you. May I introduce to you—your , PUPPY—your pastor!

May I ask you to make a decision today to ADOPT YOUR PASTOR afresh today and take your puppy/pastor home with you in your hearts and prayers?

Oh, by the way, do you know what they call pastors in Germany?
"German Shepherds"

OK, yes, it's good to laugh; it's better than medicine

Will you make a new commitment to nurture and honor your pastor with love, encouragement, and prayers in a fresh way that pleases God?

And your free gift—the pastor—needs your care and attention in order for him and the church to survive and thrive. When the pastor's needs are cared for, he can focus his attention on church leadership. Many pastors have served their best and laid down their lives for their church only to be taken for granted, or criticized, or used as the object of cruel gossip until his leadership was diminished and discarded. The church truly suffered. Don't let that happen to your pastor and church.

If a puppy needs tender loving care in order to survive, how much more your pastor needs your tender loving care, as he is shepherd to so many?

**Yes, I'm stressing a point. Please—take good care of God's gift, your pastor.**

Pastors need prayer. The Word of God reveals that God has given your pastor to you as a gift but doesn't promise a perfect gift. **Pastors are only human** with much responsibility. Pastors must rely on God for wisdom to care for the church, and to remain faithful and steadfast. Pastors need your prayers so they can be powerful and effective leaders.

We all make mistakes and sometimes, fail miserably, yet we pray for forgiveness and grace because we need to grow and become better stewards of all God has entrusted to us. Pastors are no different; they are human just like us. They experience temptation, depression, hurts, and disappointments too. After all, what is the family of God but people saved by grace, growing into the fullness of His likeness from glory to glory, together as one family!

Take good care of the gift from God, your pastor. Pray daily for him and his family.

Charles Spurgeon left us a great example for pastors and their flock. He was a great 19th-century Baptist pastor from

England. He was very intelligent and possessed great gifts of understanding and influencing people. He had a natural talent as an orator. He was an avid reader and a most prolific Christian writer as well. He had many God-given talents and was faithfully cared for, prayed for, and honored by his church.

He remained humble in spite of such fame. He captured people's hearts with his simple and sincere message of Christ's atoning work on the cross, and he had a heart to please and glorify God. Over a century later, he remains an exemplary model preacher for all pastors, and his congregation remains an exemplary model of prayer support for all pastors.

Spurgeon had a conversion experience, or a new birth, at the age of fifteen. He was drawn by the Holy Spirit, and was motivated by his passion to know God better.

Charles Spurgeon's love for God prompted him to develop a lifelong habit of rising early and spending those first hours of the day in daily Bible study, fellowship, and prayer. Consequently, he had an enormous impact on the entire world and attained great popularity and success. His message was earnest beyond description, simple yet powerful because it centered on the cross. In his life God's greatest blessings came through life's greatest challenges of sickness and persecution which kept Spurgeon humble in spite of being labeled the "Prince of Preachers." Thousands of people flocked to hear this "Prince of Preachers" preach, and his church grew.

His life was filled with Biblical instructions for Christians, especially pastors. He preached through much adversity in his own life, but kept his eyes on Christ and His gospel to save the lost.

At the age of nineteen this famous pastor's weekly messages were translated into approximately twenty languages and distributed everywhere it was humanly possible. Spurgeon often preached ten times a week to audiences of six thousand plus. Once he preached to an audience of over twenty-three thousand, without the aid of amplification. He grew the congregation of London's famed New Park Street Church. Rapid growth caused the congregation to search for larger buildings. They moved to Exeter Hall, then to Surrey Music Hall, because frequently he preached to crowds numbering more than ten thousand. Finally, due to the enormous throngs of people, a new building was constructed, and Spurgeon and the congregation voted to change the name of their church to the Metropolitan Tabernacle. It became the largest independent congregation in the world at that time.

When word of this pastor's success reached America, an official pastors' delegation was sent on a long voyage to England to visit Pastor Spurgeon. These pastors wanted to know the secret of his success and take that information back to help America's churches prosper.

After arriving in England, the American pastors were greeted by Spurgeon at his church on a late Sunday afternoon. Spurgeon had already preached two Sunday morning messages. When the opportunity arose, the pastors asked about the secret of his successful ministry. Spurgeon replied, **"Follow me."**

They were led to a room near the pulpit. When Spurgeon opened the door, the **loud roar of prayer** billowing forth overwhelmed them. This unexpected scene startled the visiting pastors for they witnessed over **four hundred**

church members praying for their pastor at four o'clock in the afternoon. The prayer warriors had been there in constant prayer since early morning, and it was now four pm.

Spurgeon spoke and pointed to the prayer warriors, "You want to know the secret of my success? <u>**My people are praying for me.**</u>"

That was it- end of conversation! He closed the door, walked away from the pastors and out of their life that quickly, despite knowing the visitors had traveled thousands of miles just to see him.

He had given them their answer. **The secret was prayer!**

While the American pastors stood there, listening in awe, two specific prayers stood out: **First, the prayer warriors were asking God to bless their pastor. Second, they were asking God to anoint their pastor as he preached later that night.** In order to accommodate the crowds, he had to preach another service that night, even though he had already preached twice that morning.

Do you know of a church where four hundred church members would give up an entire Sunday and miss all the services, just to spend time in a room praying for their pastor?

The only instance I am aware of happened over two thousand years ago. One hundred twenty followers of Christ went into an **upper room for ten consecutive days** and prayed until the Holy Spirit rushed in with great power and glory.

When will we recognize that God has chosen to move mightily through the prayers of His people?

Prayer is so powerful and accomplishes the impossible! This is why it's crucial for the house of the Lord to be and remain a house of prayer for all nations.

Pastors Need Prayer

Chapter 5
Never Criticize Your Pastor

"Let the elders who rule well be counted worthy of double honor, especially they who labor in word and doctrine" (1 Timothy 5:17) NJKV

The Bible declares that Jesus Christ our Savior is continually interceding on our behalf before God the Father—**for us.** Conversely, Satan is continually accusing before God the Father—**against us.**

In **Romans 8:34 NLT** **"Who then will condemn us? No one-for Christ Jesus Died for us and was raised for us, and He is sitting in the place of honor at God's right hand, pleading (Interceding) for us."** That's the greatest news!

However, the Bible also reveals in **Revelation 12:10 that the enemy accuses us before our God day and night.**

So, the truth is that **Jesus is interceding without ceasing and the devil is accusing without ceasing- day and night.** Satan can't read our minds or know our hearts as only God can, but he's a crafty, sly, and studious foe. We make it too easy for him because our big mouths open and reveal who we are, our thoughts, our plans and our motives.

How often do we pray this Scripture, **"Set a guard over my mouth, O LORD; keep watch over the door of my lips. Let not my heart be drawn to what is evil, to take part in wicked deeds…" (Psalm 141:3-4). NIV**

Dick Eastman shared, *"Probably the number one sin in the world, often rendering prayer ineffective is the sin of criticism, with its roots of bitterness and hate. Nothing gives Satan a free hand destroying the efforts of bended knees more than a spirit of criticism. Of all the weapons in Satan's arsenal, this one most assuredly is the greatest.* ***In truth, what prayer means to God, criticism means to Satan."***

" …who art thou that judgest another?" (James 4:12).KJV

I am about to test your patience with me by boldly encouraging you to—***shut up and pray***. Your opinions and criticisms will not change the world into a better place, but your prayers will. All of us need to shut up and pray.

I hope you still love me? I don't intend to offend; I am simply trying to make a point. **Prayer changes things—gossip and criticism don't.**

So the question is: what do you do continually? Are you praying without ceasing for your pastor, or are you joining the devil's team unknowingly and accusing your pastor with criticism?

In **I Chronicles 16:22 the bible says: "Touch not my anointed ones, do my prophets no harm."** When you speak evil of your pastor, you become an enemy of God!

Francis Frangipane shares that, *"Criticisms are a smoke screen for a prayerless heart and an unwillingness to serve."*

One of the most destructive acts in the church today is criticism. Almost nothing does more damage to the Kingdom of God.

The late great theologian and revivalist, Jonathan Edwards said, *"If some Christians that have been complaining of their pastors had said and acted less before men and applied themselves with all their might to cry to God for their pastors, had as it were risen and stormed Heaven with their humble, fervent and non-stop prayers for them, they would have been much more in the way of success."* This statement is so true.

The real truth is that the safest place to be in the entire world should be in the Christian church family.

Imagine a church where everyone decided, with the help and power of the Holy Spirit, that criticism would never be permitted. In fact, everyone diligently stood guard over their thoughts, motives, and words to never allow criticism to be spoken. Like a magnet, this would pull the unsaved people of the world to your church in droves. Your family members, neighbors, coworkers and friends would flock to your church if they knew there was such a place in their city, a place where people showed the authentic love of God at all times.

Yes, your church should be the safest place on earth. But is it?

What if someone drove up to your church in a most luxurious

car, wearing expensive, name-brand clothes, and was quite prestigious with a great reputation? How would you treat that person compared to a poor person who walked to your church wearing dirty, stinky, torn clothes, who was unkempt and looked peculiar, certainly not like everybody else. Would you treat them the same?

Can you honestly say in your heart of hearts that you would gravitate to the person with more visible needs, or would you favor the well-dressed person with first-class treatment hoping they would join your church? How would you feel if you were the poor person shunned and rejected? What would you think of Christians?

If you have lived long enough, you have felt the sting of criticism. You may have heard someone you cared for criticize you when he or she thought you weren't present. You may have been the subject of someone's displeasure as he or she spoke in secret to a friend, but it eventually reached your ears. You may have received this criticism face to face. I think we have all been there at some point in our lives and know it really hurts.

As I write these words I am thinking of a great pastor friend across town who is so down and discouraged. Everytime God gives the church a breakthrough in the community outreach, there are members who constantly criticise the pastor and the leadership. This has happened so many times and after years of this it becomes almost unbearable.

"But why dost thou judge thy brother?" (Romans 14:10).
KJV

For most of my preaching engagements, I've received many encouraging compliments regarding my message and ministry. **However, there are times** I've received a critical complaint. Why is it that one complaint lingered with me and hurt for awhile until I took it before the Lord and asked for help in getting over it? My wise and sweet wife Dee would say in her charming style, "Honey, you received all of those great words from so many people, so why do you let one criticism hurt you and affect you that way?" I would reply, "It just really hurts." **Are you aware that the number one day for pastors' to resign the ministry is on Mondays?** This is the day that they receive the criticisms for their preaching and teaching from the weekend. I counsel pastors to never open their emails or any anonymous letters until Tuesday.

The next time you open your lips to criticize, try to remember what it feels like when it happens to you and offer up loving prayers instead. You will feel so much better, and it will so please the Lord hearing you show godly love to your pastor.

Criticism never helps, builds or encourages. It does the exact opposite. It hurts, tears down, and discourages. We need to make a decision to never criticize our pastor ever again. In fact, we should never criticize anyone ever again. We need to declare it against the law! Are you willing to take this watchful and committed stand?

Ask the Lord right now to help you control the words flowing from your mouth. Remember that what comes out of your mouth is an outflow of what's in your heart. The Bible reveals, "...**For out of the abundance of the heart the mouth speaks" (Matthew 12:34, NKJV).** So, ask the Lord for an inside out change of heart and submit to the Holy Spirit's lead. He is faithful to hear your prayer and will help you be victorious.

By obeying the Holy Spirit's prompts, you won't criticize your pastor again, but if anyone starts down that dingy road with you, gently lead that person in another direction. But first share the truth with honest humility, "Say to them I'm sorry you made that comment. I've been asking the Lord to help me avoid all criticism, and I'm asking you to please refrain from saying anything like that to me again. I'm not perfect and have made mistakes in the past, but I'm trying to change. Please understand my heart, and let's talk about something else."

I doubt that friend will ever try that again because your message will be very clear. This is a great way to develop an environment free of criticism. Also the church could teach a Bible study centered on the ill-effects of criticism to lead people out of this darkness, followed by a Bible study on the gift of love described in **1 Corinthians, Chapter 13. So don't remain in the darkness with hurtful, critical words. Turn to the light and love of God and walk in it.**

Love is what shouts to the world we are Christians, for God is love. In fact the source and foundation of prayer should be God's love. Showing God's love changes people and circumstances. God showed His love by offering forgiveness for our many sins, including our hurtful and critical words, through Jesus' sacrificial act of love and obedience to His Father. That blessing of obedience extended forgiveness to the whole world; it offered God's love to the world. We believers are to act in the same manner that will bring the same result. Don't you want that same blessing that comes from obedience?

Yes, God's will is for His people to never criticize anyone or act in any malicious manner, and to always obey His Word and Spirit, but true justice, fairness, and recompense won't happen on the earth. Why?

Because believers are on a personal journey of transformation that will be perfected and finished by Jesus as we enter heaven one day. Only Jesus will make it right on that day.

As Christ's followers, even when we are stung by criticism, we are all to forgive quickly, and follow Jesus' example. The Holy Spirit leads us this way to accomplish God's will for us right now. We don't want to be stuck in unforgiveness and hurt, for it will cause us to miss the current opportunity and blessing that is just behind that door of forgiveness. I would like to recommend a wonderful book called, "Total Forgiveness" by R.T. Kendall. This book has impacted many thousands of readers, including myself. In his book he states: *"Forgiveness is the road to the greater anointing"*.

Forgiveness opens the door to God's light, love, and possibilities for you and others around you, even those you don't know. Our words and actions have long-range capabilities to affect those we don't even know, but those whom God loves.

Love equals obedience—to God's Word; it shouts love to Jesus and others. When we put a guard on our lips, we can amaze Jesus. Even when others don't and criticize us, we can amaze Jesus by yielding to the Holy Spirit inside to forgive the hurt quickly, before the sun goes down. Let's amaze Jesus with our love as we yield and submit to the Holy Spirit and only speak words that point others to Him. Let's forgive quickly.

However, make it a point today and every day to speak lovely, pure and noble words of good report. This obedience has a twofold blessing for it speaks love to God and love to our neighbor. **Honor your pastor and love each other this way instead of criticizing.**

Instead of allowing critical words to erupt like a volcano, take them to the Lord in prayer, and pray for change. Then praise God. This blesses your pastor and you. It opens your heart toward your pastor to receive his messages centered on the gospel of Christ. Prayer instead of criticism will restore unity within the church. Remember, it's not about the pastor or us. It's all about Jesus and living His way for His glory! **Seek His face today and remain in His presence. You will remain in His supernatural peace.**

<u>WARNING TO INTERCESSORS</u>

Sometimes in your private prayer times the Lord might occasionally show you an area in your pastor that needs prayer. (**This is for prayer only**) Never, Ever, share this information or even hint to others that God has shown you anything. This is for you to lovingly and humbly pray for your pastor. Many pastors have been critically wounded by so-called prayer warriors who spread lies and secret rumors all in the name of prayer. Don't do it. Stay quiet and humble. What if everyone knew all your private secrets? If the Lord chooses to share these areas with you, He is trusting you to take them to His throne in prayer. Be faithful and never criticize your pastor!

Ted Rose

Chapter 6
Pray Daily For Your Pastor

"...Men ought always to pray, and not to faint" (Luke 18:1). KJV

Bill Bright, the late Founder and President of Campus Crusade for Christ, commented, *"No segment of our society is more strategic and more in need of prayer than pastors and their families. They urgently and desperately need our love, encouragement and earnest prayers."*

How can you help? By looking to Jesus. our perfect example for effective prayer. He rose early and set aside quiet time specifically to pray. Jesus, our Lord and Savior, God in the flesh—rose early to pray. You can follow in His footsteps.

As you depend on the Holy Spirit's lead, organize each day to include prayer at a specific time. Create a daily plan for powerful prayers. Commit to meet with Jesus in prayer, eager to spend precious moments with Him. God is faithful and will answer.

It's important to set aside a specific time each day to pray, kneeling in prayer to meet with God. However, the thought that you don't have to get down on your knees to pray may cross your mind. True, you can pray on the way to work or anywhere, but nothing takes the place of a special prayer time each day focused on your Lord and Saviour.

During this quiet and uninterrupted time, you can also present a list of petitions to your Heavenly Father in the throne room of God.

From these intimate and secluded moments in the prayer closet, you can receive revelations that illuminate your life beyond those received while praying and driving **65 miles-an-hour** on your way to work. These revelations can transform your life and your pastor's life here on earth. The prayer closet is an essential asset to every believer's Christian walk. One author on prayer said, "The man who does not set a specific time to pray each day, will not pray!" Having spent over thirty years teaching and preaching on prayer, I can say that this is so true.

To trust in the Holy Spirit's guidance as you develop a daily habit of prayer is of ultimate importance; it's the key to breakthroughs.

Webster defines: *habit: as a pattern of action that is acquired and has become so automatic that it's difficult to break.*

Research has proven that a particular habit is formed after being repeated twenty-one times consecutively. You are twenty-one days away from a spectacular revolution in your prayer life. You may alter the destiny of countless souls, encourage pastors, and help change the world.

Prayer is the key to unleashing the power of God to bring about amazing breakthroughs.

Here is a poem that is a call from the Lord to the church to be a true House of Prayer for All Nations, so that he will have a house to pour out His love and healing to the world:

House of Prayer

By Ted Rose

House of Prayer
Where is your incense?
House of Prayer
Where is your travail?

House of Prayer
Where is your intercession?
House of Prayer
You must not fail!

House of Prayer,
I need your commitment.
House of Prayer
I need you to weep.

House of Prayer
I want you to awaken!
House of Prayer
No more to sleep.

House of Prayer
Full of mighty men,
House of Prayer

Pastors Need Prayer

Draw near to war.

A House of Prayer
Is what I called you to be,
A House of Prayer
Forever more!

In **Luke 18:1,KJV** Jesus reveals, **"...Men ought always to pray, and not to faint."** The Son of God commands every believer to pray and not faint. What does this mean exactly?

Let's take a further look at this very important verse. The word always in the Greek language is *πάντοτε or pantote, which means—at all times, ever, never ceasing.*

Does the Son of God actually want every believer to pray continually at all times? The answer is a resounding *yes*! Most believers agree it's a good idea to pray but wouldn't necessarily believe in non-stop prayers. But Jesus' own words reveal that it's not a suggestion but a directive, a command.

What about fainting? What does Jesus mean by that? The word faint in the Greek language is *ἐκκακέω or ekkakeō, which means—to be utterly spiritless, to be wearied out, exhausted, to be weak, to fail in heart, without courage, vigor or enthusiasm, halfhearted.* One of the inferences is that to faint in prayer shows a flaw or difficulty in one's character.

George Mueller, the great preacher and founder of one of the most successful ministries for orphans commented, *"I live in the spirit of prayer. I pray as I walk about, when I lie down and when I rise up. And the answers are always coming.* ***Thousands and tens of thousands of times have my prayers been answered.*** *When once I am persuaded that a thing is* *right and for the glory of God, I go on praying for it until the answer comes."*

A reporter once asked George Mueller, *"Has ever God not answered one of your prayers?"* To that question brother Mueller suddenly jumped to his feet and loudly exclaimed, *"Never, God always answers my prayers!" He then went on to say, "However, I have been praying for my friend's son to come to Jesus for sixty-two years and three months. He is not saved yet, but he will be! How can it be otherwise, for George Mueller is praying."*

It is a historical recorded fact that after George Mueller died and was being lowered into the grave, his friend's son finally gave his life to Jesus Christ right there at the gravesite. George prayed all those years for him: and victoriously, his prayer was answered, as yours will be too. Sixty-two years plus of praying for one request without receiving a quick answer is putting the words of Jesus faithfully into action—**to pray and never give up, and not faint or grow weary.**

Please remember that when it seems your prayers are worthless and unheard, there is victory ahead. If you remain patient, steadfast and diligent to pray, the results will be victorious even though sometimes you may not see it here on earth. Know deep in your heart that your prayers bring blessings to people, to your loved ones today, and for generations to come. Prayers are powerful to change people's lives. My Director of Ministry Relations, Mindy Flynn, coined a phrase years ago, when she said: **"God doesn't answer Email, just <u>Knee</u> mail.**

God is touched and moved by your faith. Prayers show your faith in God, that you depend on Him and trust Him to accomplish the impossible. Prayers are powerful to transform people, places, and events.

Another truly amazing fact is that George Mueller had several prayer journals that contained over **33,000 names** of people for whom he was asked to pray. People had sent him names of loved ones in hopes he would pray for their salvations. **After George Mueller's passing, research found that every one of these 33,000 people came to Jesus Christ. His prayers had truly amazing results—but so do yours!**

George Mueller used to say, ***"The greatest secret to prayer is to never ever give up."*** I truly believe that many who pray don't continue with a steadfast confidence that God will answer them. What if Daniel had given up after twelve days instead of praying continually until he received his breakthrough of victory?

E.M. Bounds, the late and great prayer mobilizer said, *"Our praying needs to be pressed and pursued with an energy that never tires, a persistence which will not be denied, and a courage which never fails. If the church wants a better pastor, it only needs to pray for the one it has."*

John Wesley said, *"God does nothing apart from prayer, but he does everything by it."*

So, you might be asking, what type of commitment to prayer is needed? That is a great question. **To truly obey the word of God, we all need to become walking, talking, breathing and praying houses of prayer.** We should make a commitment to pray every day for our pastor.

Will you commit to being diligent in prayer times for your pastor? If so, you and your pastor will see great results and accomplish great things for the Lord. You can be transformed into a mighty prayer warrior. The Lord can take you on a lifelong journey of exciting prayer, if you allow. What could possibly be better than to be welcomed before the throne of God? It's your privilege and honor to spend time in the presence of God. He wants your petitions. He wants your worship and love. Incredible joy arises as you realize God has blessed people because of your prayers.

As you pray for your pastor, think of ways to show support. Pastors desire kindnesses similar to those you extend to other friends. Why not send a card every month with an encouraging note inside? A simple yet positive thought shared with your pastor can assure him you are praying for him. It will brighten his day. You cannot imagine what an impact a simple note of blessing will do.

Show your faithfulness. Make no mistake about it; Satan hates it when you pray.

You're not just fighting your own flesh when you attempt to pray, but you're fighting the enemy of your soul. The devil doesn't really mind if you go to church, read your Bible, and call yourself a Christian. But he hates it when you pray. He knows that when you pray, you call upon the mighty power of God. In any situation, **prayer unleashes spiritual, nuclear-tipped, ballistic missiles against the kingdom of darkness.**

However, remember that when you move from one level of prayer to a life overflowing with daily intercessory prayer, you can expect opposition from the enemy. Even so, there is no need to fear. God is in control. God is the only one to fear. Remain steadfast in prayer, fixed on God, and desiring to please Him. The Bible doesn't say that you will be sheltered from attacks. In fact, quite the opposite is true. The Bible clearly portrays our spiritual battle.

"For we wrestle not against flesh and blood, but against principalities, against powers, against the rulers of the darkness of this world, against spiritual wickedness in high places" (Ephesians 6:12).KJV

The revivalist, Leonard Ravenhill, stated, *"Men of prayer*

must be men of steel, for they will be assaulted by Satan even before they attempt to assault his kingdom." Yes, your enemy furiously and tirelessly works to steal your faith and your belief in God. Satan doesn't want you to realize the power that is yours through prayer in Jesus' name.

The great news is that the Bible declares, **"...Greater is He that is in you, than he that is in the world" (1 John 4:4). KJV** This is the assurance from the Lord that you have a greater source of power within you so you have no need to fear! He gives you guidance and encouragement to remain steadfast and rely on God's greater power, the Holy Spirit within, and claim your victory as God always wins!

My heart's prayer for you is that when you finish reading this book, you'll hear the voice of God calling you to the place of prayer. In the book of **Revelation,** the Word of God says over and over, **"He that hath an ear, let him hear what the Spirit says to the churches." Revelation 2:17 NKJV**

I pray that your ears will be open and sensitive to the voice of the Spirit of God and hear the clarion call to the church. Come into the prayer chamber and sup with the Lord in intimacy and intercession.

Most people have never heard of the prayer support of Evangelist Reinhard Bonnke, the Evangelist to Africa who has had Crusades with record attendees of over 2.5 million people in a single meeting. They have recorded over 1.5 million written commitments of salvation in one gathering. What causes such fruit and success? Well, Reinhard Bonnke knows that unless there is enough prayer, nothing will happen. But, if God's people pray, then the strongholds of the Devil will be broken and many people will accept Christ. So, a woman of God, named Suzette Hattingh, is the one who has overseen the prayer ministry for the ministry for 16 years. She, along with 5,000 intercessors, pray for months before every Crusade, praying hours every day, using verses of Scripture as their guide for prayer. Then after months of pre-prayer, they arrive at the crusade location and they go into either a building set up on location or a prayer tent- 5,000 dedicated believers calling upon the Lord in prayer. They pray for hours at a time, before, during, and after each crusade service. Meanwhile, outside millions come to Jesus. Do you want to see awesome, powerful results through the ministry of your Pastor and local Church? Then believe and commit to daily prayer at a level you have never done before and then look out because the Lord is faithful and He will do it.

After reading this book you will never be able to say that you did not know that God wanted you to pray. Please remember that it is your responsibility to pray as a believer in the Lord Jesus Christ, and effectively change lives. **Every believer is called to prayer.**

Pastors Need Prayer

Chapter 7
Become an Armor Bearer in Prayer for Your Pastor

"But Moses' hands were heavy; and they took a stone, and put it under him, and he sat thereon; and Aaron and Hur stayed up his hands, the one on the one side, and the other on the other side; and his hands were steady until the going down of the sun." (Exodus 17: 12). KJV

"And David came to Saul, and stood before him. And he loved him greatly, and became his armorbearer" (1 Samuel 16:21). NKJV

Pastor Chuck Swindoll said, *"We need to remember that prayer is battle, it wages war not against God but against the status quo, against sin and fallenness and the flesh and devils."*

Samuel Chadwick wrote, *"This praying will not retreat until all of Satan's demons are moved aside, heaven's gates are opened, and God's promises are poured forth."*

Your pastor needs you as his spiritual armor bearer. This need is revealed in many places throughout the Bible. God has shown and established both dependence on Him and inter-dependence on one another. **Dick Eastman, President of the worldwide ministry of Every Home for Christ, has listed three unalterable convictions in their mission statement.**

     1- **The Great Commission is to be taken literally.**
     2- **We can't do this alone; we need each other.**
     3- **Prayer alone is what will remove all obstacles.**

This ministry has used these fundamental principles to win over 128 Million souls to the Lord since 1953. The Lord has built into the Kingdom of God a need for one another. Your pastor cannot accomplish his ministry without God-sent co-laborers and supporters in prayer. Prayer is the most important element for achieving any breakthrough or success. The degree of success for your pastor is the degree to which prayer is utilized and mobilized.

Have you noticed that Jesus didn't send His disciples out alone–ever? He always sent them out in teams of two or more. Why did he do this? He did it because of the need for teamwork and inter-dependence.

Throughout history when God used a godly man or woman in a powerful way—to change mankind's destiny—he or she would have faithful people praying for them. For example, take the ministry of Charles Finney, one of the greatest evangelists in America's history. Pastor Father Daniel Nash and Abel Clary left the pulpit ministry to devote their lives to prayer for Charles Finney and the revival that was impacting our nation. These two men would go before all of Finney's crusades, locate a room in a home, barn or basement, and spend hours every day and night agonizing and weeping in prayer for men's lost souls.

However, these men never attended a Finney meeting. They knew their role was to pray. When they heard that the outpouring of the Spirit of God was being released and souls were coming to Christ, then they quietly moved to the next town or village, Nash and Clary began to pray for that new region until the presence of God would come there also. For seven years they prayed faithfully for Finney's ministry, constantly moving from one town to another.

In the seven years that Father Nash and brother Clary spent praying for the revival, **over 1,250,000 souls came to Jesus Christ**. In addition, **eighty percent** of these new Christians remained steadfast in their faith through death. That was an unprecedented statistic. Even Charles Moody's percentage was only fifty percent.

Three or four months after Father Nash died, Charles Finney left the revival ministry to become a pastor of a local church. Finney did this because he had no one else who was willing to pay the price in prayer like his friend, Father Nash.

You see every Charles Finney needs a Father Nash. Billy Graham had Armin Geswein, Reinhart Bonke had Suzette Hattingh, and Dr. Youngi Cho had Mama Choi.

Reverend Samuel Rodriguez, president of the National Hispanic Christian Leadership Conference of over 40,000 Churches in America, has given me the honor of praying as his Chief Intercessor. My responsibility or mission is to live in prayer hours every day for this man of God and to mobilize a national prayer team to support this ministry. Why? We want to impact millions to know Christ, and help change the world.

Reverend Rodriguez has an open door to pray for presidents

in the White House and brings the presence of God to the highest parts of our government. No leader can do it alone; he needs a team who prays to accomplish his mission.

I am also blessed to have full-time prayer warriors praying for me all these years, beloved armor bearers who have stood with me through all the storms of life because I cannot do it alone either. I need to share with you, that without these faithful intercessors praying for my family and me, we never would have made it.

The story of my son who was shot and killed:
Last year my 24 year old son **"Johnny"** was shot and killed. He was killed while in my loving arms. Johnny was the most loving, sweet young man that I have ever known. His honesty, loyalty and tenderness made me a better man. I cannot tell you how much I miss him. This totally devastated me and my entire family. Truly this was the darkest moment of our life and souls. We were not prepared for what happened next. The Body of Christ around the world came to our side and lifted us up in prayer like never before. We were carried each day before the Throne of Grace and help to receive strength and healing. We are so grateful to everyone who prayed us through. Now we are able to minister to those that experience the sorrow and pain of a tragic and sometimes gruesome loss. We need each other as we go through lifes challenges and toughest moments.

Leaders never lead by themselves.
A most inspirational story in the Bible is the story of Moses in Exodus. Moses unified and mobilized others against the Amalekites at Rephidim when they attacked the Israelites.

"Moses said to Joshua, **'Choose some of our men and go**

92

out to fight the Amalekites. Tomorrow I will stand on top of the hill with the staff of God in my hands.'

So Joshua fought the Amalekites as Moses had ordered, and Moses, Aaron and Hur went to the top of the hill. As long as Moses held up his hands, the Israelites were winning, but whenever he lowered his hands, the Amalekites were winning. When Moses' hands grew tired, they took a stone and put it under him and he sat on it. Aaron and Hur held his hands up—one on one side, one on the other—so that his hands remained steady till sunset. So Joshua overcame the Amalekite army with the sword" (Exodus 17:9-13). NIV

It's important to remember that as long as Moses's hands were lifted up, the Israelites were winning. **Winning means that the Amalekites died. But when His hands fell down, the Israelites died.**

Supporting your pastor in prayer and holding up his arms as an Aaron and Hur, which is an armor bearer, is a matter of **life and death.** You help make the difference as to whether your pastor is a success or a failure. Success in this instance means the people that your pastor cares for will have victory in their lives and circumstances. You might be thinking, you mean by me praying for my pastor every day, it will actually impact the many lives he ministers too? The answer is yes. It is up to you.

What is an armor bearer? The Bible mentions the position of armor bearer numerous times. In studying both the Bible and history, we find that not everyone was given an armor bearer. So who could receive a dedicated armor bearer?

All kings and soldiers of distinction were allocated a

personal armor bearer. However, not every soldier received one, because the workers were few.

What was the role of the armor bearer? It was to provide all of the needs of the one to whom they were assigned. The armor bearer attended to personal needs, such as food and clothing, and oversaw the armor and weapons of their leader. Perhaps the most important role of the armor bearer was to protect during the heat of battle. The armor bearer had in his possession a large shield, so large that when lifted in battle it would cover the armor bearer and the soldier of distinction.

The armor bearer would go out in front of his leader and carry the shield to help the soldier move forward under the protection of the shield. The armor bearer would **never abandon their leader** but would be willing to die before quitting or leaving.

How many pastors have been left heartbroken by individuals who once said that the Lord sent them to help? How many pastors have watched people leave because they, the pastors, didn't do exactly as was requested by the armor bearers? Where are the faithful, humble, and courageous servants of God who will stay through thick and thin?

Get your shield out, for the Bible instructs, **"In addition to all this, take up the shield of faith, with which you can extinguish all the flaming arrows of the evil one" (Ephesians 6:16, NIV).**

The enemy is firing fiery darts at you and your pastor. But if you take out your powerful shield, you can stand in intercession for others and deflect those darts so they won't hurt those whom you are defending.

Maybe you haven't had your shield out for awhile. Get it out, dust it off, and start wielding it with confidence and power and cause some damage to the kingdom of darkness. Protect your leader! Make the declaration that if the devil wants to attack your pastor, then he will have to go through the Jesus within you first, and we know that is not possible. Remember, **"...Greater is He that is in you than he that is in the world" (1 John 4:4). KJV**

Your vision is my vision.
Make a commitment to God to support the vision of your pastor, and tell him so. You could say something like this, "Your vision is my vision. From this moment on, I am with you. How may I serve and help you accomplish what the Lord has put into your heart?" When you unite with your pastor's vision, that spiritual unity produces spiritual synergy; your pastor reaps the harvest of blessings you sowed from your obedient, loving prayers and you reap the harvest of blessings your pastor sowed from his obedient, loving service to God and His church. This glories Abba Father, the Lord Jesus Christ and the Holy Spirit .

Story of Christian, the Armor Bearer
I would like to share a true story with you. One Sunday morning as I was teaching at a church on the subject of "Adopting Your Pastor in Prayer," I decided to use some members of the congregation to demonstrate and illustrate a portion of my teaching. Several big and strong-looking men were called up to be armor bearers. I had the pastor stand in the altar of the church with these large men surrounding him. Then I looked out into the crowd to find someone to play the role of Satan. I called out a young man to play the enemy and asked his name. He replied, "Christian!" Laughter erupted and filled the church.

Out of all the people in this huge crowd, the one guy I chose to play the devil was named Christian. What are the chances of that happening? As the laughter faded, we continued. I asked all of the armor bearers to unite and stand together. Under no circumstances were they to allow the enemy to break through their defenses to reach the pastor.

I then told Christian, our acting devil, to do everything in his power to reach and destroy the pastor. The war began. Christian charged the armor bearers, who were defending the pastor, with all his might. He tried his best to reach the pastor, but he couldn't even break through the armor bearers first line defense. They were committed to ensuring that no one could touch their pastor. It turned out to be a very powerful illustration to everyone of the role that we have as prayer warriors and armor bearers for our pastors.

I received an unexpected phone call from the same pastor a few months later. He asked, "Do you remember the man named Christian, who role played as the devil on that Sunday? "Yes," I replied. "Well, your illustration has changed Christian's life."

The pastor informed me of the impact that illustration had on Christian's life and how it prompted him to become his personal armor bearer attending to his needs as a loyal helper. "Furthermore," he continued, "Christian is also now leading prayer for me in our church as well. His whole life has changed since he role-played the enemy who was locked in intense battle charging toward his pastor." The pastor and I rejoiced and gave God praise together. Terry Nance, wrote a great book that I would like to recommend to you called: "God's Armor Bearer".

Servant's Heart for your Pastor

Humility not only pleases God, but it also entreats the Spirit of God to move and flow in your direction. The Bible says, "... **God resists the proud, but He gives grace to the humble" (James 4:6).** NKJV The word "grace" as used here has the same definition that the Lord used in his invitation to the throne. He said, **"Let us therefore come boldly unto the throne of grace, that we may obtain mercy, and find grace to help in time of need." (Hebrews 4:16) KJV**

When praying for others, ask God for grace, redemption, and hope as well as a second chance. Remember, it's humility that attracts God's attention.

Traits or Attributes of an Armor Bearer:
At the end of this chapter, I have presented many different traits and attributes of an armor bearer. Please review them and remember the importance of developing traits you may not have. This is not an all-inclusive list, but plenty to think about. There may be several attributes listed that you could focus on for improvement. This process doesn't happen overnight. If many of the traits below are your strengths, praise the Lord. If there are some areas of weakness, please humbly ask the Lord to strengthen you and believe that He will.

Remain faithful in your role as an armor bearer. Rest assured, you will see your pastor have moments of weakness. **You will see his humanity, and your commitment will be tested.** As long as your pastor does your will and makes the right decisions according to your agenda, it's very easy to follow and serve him. However, when he makes a mistake or proceeds against what you think is right, will you still be faithful to him? Its time for all of us to grow up and not be so self-sensitive. Be strong, stable and faithful.

I know it isn't easy. But remember—you make mistakes too. Would you want people to walk away from you because you make a mistake? Nobody wants that. So give grace to your pastor, and treat him the way you want to be treated. Staying through the hard times isn't easy, but its rewards are so sweetly worth it.

Armor Bearer Traits

- Broken
- Contrite
- Realistic
- Faithful
- Secure
- Confidential
- Understanding
- Humble
- Non-Critical
- Positive
- Helpful
- Patient
- Tireless
- Friendly
- Humorous
- Hopeful
- Persistent
- Joyful
- Practical
- Peaceful
- Loyal
- Tender
- Bold
- Courageous

- Hardworking
- Optimistic
- Determined
- Wise
- Unselfish
- Loving
- Poised
- Teachable
- Kind
- Polite
- Biblical
- Prayerful
- Forgiving
- Strong
- Diligent
- Sacrificial
- Resourceful
- Energetic
- Honest
- Integrity
- Disciple
- Stable
- Discerning
- Alert
- Servant Heart
- Dependable
- Tactful
- Sensitive
- Valiant
- Trustworthy
- Inspiring
- Watchful
- Resilient
- Caring
- Warrior

Pastors Need Prayer

- Perseptive

Chapter 8
How to Pray for Your Pastor

"The effectual fervent prayer of a
righteous man availeth much" (James 5:16). KJV

Reverend Billy Graham said, *"If you do not feel like praying, it is probably a good indication that you should start praying immediately."*

Most people don't realize that the inner circle of the Billy Graham Evangelistic Association doesn't call their crusades Evangelistic Crusades. They are called **Prayer Crusades.** Why? Because they know that unless there is a serious campaign of prayer preceding each crusade, there won't be an effective gathering of the harvest. In fact, any city that wants their presence is required to spend over a year in a unified, massive prayer effort before they arrive to preach the gospel.

One of the great experiences of my life was when I served as Chairman of the Prayer Committee for the Luis Palau Sacramento City Festival. Along with my amazing and truly special Co-Chair, Annie Fish, we began to pray together and ask the Lord to give us a plan and a strategy. He did. The Lord impressed upon us to develop a region-wide team of Christians who would commit to prayer every day for the upcoming festival. **We recruited over four thousand intercessors, and we prayed for one full year in advance.** We had special city-wide prayer meeting. All night prayer meetings. Prayer Conference Calls. Prayer alerts went out every month. Prayer was taking place everywhere. We prayed at the location where the City Festival would be taking place. We had prayer walks all over the city. We believed that when the thousands upon thousands gathered at the festival to hear the gospel preached by Dr. Luis Palau, the International Christian Evangelist, we would see many come to Christ. God gave us promises in His word that if we would pray he would come!

That's exactly what happened. When the invitations were given, thousands came to Christ. We collected the names of those who made their commitments to the Lord, and we have been praying over their names ever since.

Do you see the powerful impact of prayer? Any man or woman of God can't accomplish God's purposes alone. They need other people and their prayers to be successful. Day and night prayer is needed from believers who will never give up as they plead the promises of God. The bible says **"Shall not God avenge His own elect, which cry day and night unto Him". (Luke 18:7) KJV**

Prayer is so transforming—**it's the only thing the disciples ever asked the Lord to teach them—to pray.**

The disciples didn't ask Jesus to teach them how to preach,

how to heal the sick or how to build a church or ministry. The disciples asked Jesus to teach them how to pray. The disciples had been Jesus' followers for over three years when they asked. In **Luke 11:1, KJV, the disciples asked, "...Lord, teach us to pray..."** They understood that Jesus was and still is the only one who could do that. **Jesus alone is the Master Teacher.**

May I invite you to come to the throne room of God Almighty and sit at the feet of Jesus, the Master Teacher, and let Him teach you to pray? One of the most honest and effective prayers is to confess on a regular basis, "Father, I don't know how to pray as I should, I have so much to learn. Please teach me how to pray."

I can promise that the Holy Spirit will do this as it's according to His will. He never refuses to answer prayer according to His will, and we know He longs for us to pray. This type of prayer will launch you into a more effective level of prayer. If you and I can remain teachable and humble, He will do exceedingly abundantly above all that we can think or imagine.

Pray about prayer

A good friend, Dave Butts, President of Harvest Evangelism, and Chairman of America's Prayer Committee, is a respected national and international prayer leader. He gave one of the most important secrets to every believer or prayer leader of a church who is serious about praying. He said, *"Before you begin your prayer strategy or plan, first pray about prayer."* What he is so wisely saying is—before you finalize your system of prayer, go before the Lord and ask Him to show you His strategy and His plan. The Lord desires to give you His custom plan based upon who you or your church is through Him. His plan is always better than ours. The question is—do you really believe that the Lord will show you and speak to your heart His plan for your prayers? This will allow the Holy Spirit to be in control and lead you according to the will of God. This is very important.

Here is a poem that attempts to express the longing in our Fathers' heart to have intimate fellowship with you, as His precious beloved:

Come Away My Beloved
by Ted Rose

Come, come away my beloved
Come to the place of prayer

Come, come away my beloved
I will meet you there

Come, come away my beloved
There is so much for you to see

Come, come away my beloved
To the place of intimacy with me

Pray Regularly

I would encounter you to keep a prayer journal, including

your list of prayer requests for your pastor. This is a helpful tool of encouragement as you see your prayers being answered. A prayer journal can help you stay organized in your prayer times. After you list your prayer requests and then after praying over them for some time and then they are answered. This will strengthen your faith. It's encouraging to write down impressions received from the Holy Spirit.

Pray the Word of God

Remember when you pray to fill your prayers with the Word of God. There is nothing more powerful than praying the promises of God's Word. When you pray the Word of God, you are wielding the Sword of the Spirit. This is what defeats our enemy and enforces the victory of the cross in the name of Jesus. Pull out your sword and wield it skillfully and boldly. Be courageous, watch the victory take place, and give glory to the Lord for what he has done.

Your prayers don't have to be beautiful, fancy or eloquent in your opinion. God looks upon your heart and responds to a sincere belief in Him. Do you remember earlier in the book where we described the story of Pastor Charles Spurgeon's 400 intercessors who were heard praying two specific prayers. One was **"God bless our pastor"**, the second was **"God anoint our pastor** as he preaches the word". If you don't know how or what to pray you can simply pray these prayers. "God bless my pastor, and God anoint my pastor. He is waiting for you to call upon His name. He has said in His word in **Jeremiah 33:3, KJV,"Call to Me, and I will answer you, and show you great and mighty things which you do not know."** God is patiently inviting us to call upon His name. Think of it, He is daring us to call upon Him so that he can accomplish His will in the earth, just as it is in

Heaven.

Pray for God's Heart

Ask God to give you His heart for your pastor. I have pleaded many times to have the heart of God when I pray. Ask Him to remove the selfish heart of stone and replace with His tender heart. Ask God to give you a sensitive heart for your pastor, and that you would be available when his crisis moment arrives. Pray that you would be sensitive to the Holy Spirit's leads and prompts, and go before the Lord in prayer at that moment. You will never realize the full impact of your prayers and what they could mean at that critical moment. We all need to grow, mature, and develop this sensitivity for others and their needs by listening more to the indwelling Holy Spirit.

Pray for Family

To effectively pray for your pastor, you must understand his heart. If you were to ask your pastor to identify his number one prayer request, he most likely would respond, "Pray for my family."

In all my years of praying for pastors and other spiritual leaders, the number one request I've received is to pray for their families.

Many Christians think that pastors might want them to pray for larger congregations, larger churches, or for other areas of ministry. However, the number one concern of pastors is truly their families who are constantly under attack from the enemy. Of course when pastors' families are under attack, so are the pastors. So every day, please take a moment to pray for your pastor's marriage and family. Pray that God will bless them and protect them at all times.

Pray for a Godly Servant

After you pray for your pastor's family, please be sure to pray that your pastor will be a godly servant of the Lord and remain faithful to the call of God in their lives. Pray for your pastor to show integrity and honesty in every area of life, and for discernment and protection from ungodly and unbelieving men who desire to harm him.

Pray for your pastors' ministry

Also, please pray for your pastor's ministry. Ask God to anoint your pastor, and for his preaching and teaching to be centered on the Word of God, penetrating hearts. Pray that the congregation or church family will grow in their walk with Christ. Pray that the Holy Spirit will add to the church everyday those that should be saved. Pray that as your pastor teaches the Word of God, seeds sowed would take root and bear great fruit.

Counter the Enemy's Attacks

Your prayers make a huge difference. Have you ever experienced a satanic attack waged against your mind? You may have noticed it as a sudden wave of oppression or gloom propelling you into moments of great despair—for no apparent reason. This is an attack from the enemy. Satan targets your pastor continually with such attacks to defeat your pastor and cause him to be less effective in his role as shepherd. Even though you suffer persecutions, pastors can experience these attacks to a greater extent and volume because of the sheer number of souls they shepherd.

Everyone, including pastors, must continually rely on and trust in Jesus totally to lift our burdens when we give them to Him in obedience. We all need to yield to the Holy Spirit directing us to cast our cares on Jesus every moment. We all need to keep our eyes on Jesus instead of the circumstances racing toward us, encircling us and covering our world with darkness and despair. Just beyond the ominous clouds are the promises Jesus is waiting for us to see, but we will miss if our eyes remain on the dark moments. Don't look at this darkness, look beyond it—at the light found in the face of Jesus.

Yes, we all go astray like lost sheep, and God knew He must teach us how to think correctly so we can stay in His peace, light and joy. That's why He gave us a model for thinking found in Philippians.

I would urge everyone to read **Philippians 4:4-13;** as our thoughts fill much of our time and can bring us peace or dis-ease, light or darkness, joy or despair, victory or defeat. It all depends on whether we obey God and think the way He tells us to think in this chapter or not.

However, unless you've been a pastor, you'll never truly know or understand what it's like to be one.

A glamorous life of attention and praise it's not. As Jesus said to all of us, **"...Take up [your] cross daily, and follow Me" (Luke 9:23)**. **NKJV** Carrying this burden can remain a heavy weight no matter how much time is spent on vacation. It's a heavy burden that can crush your pastor if he doesn't give all of it to the Lord immediately, and continuously, as He instructs.

That is why your prayers are crucially important. Pray for your pastor to effectively cast his burdens on Christ and leave them there, so he can go about his business of serving the Lord and His church with joy and peace. Please ask God to bless your pastor with a refreshing wave of strength from God's Word to counter the attacks of the enemy by leaning on and trusting in Jesus for deliverance and revelation.

I have developed a prayer guide called, *Pray For My Pastor*, to help believers develop their own Biblical pattern of prayer. This prayer guide has been translated into many different languages. It is part of the *Pray for Pastors' Initiative*, which now has believers in over one hundred nations participating.

Pray For My Pastor
Prayer Guide

Please remember to pray for God's heart towards your pastor. Leave the complaints behind, and serve him with love through the ministry of prayer. He is worthy of double honor. Pray for him when you wake up, before every meal, and before you go to sleep. Ask God to help you make that commitment and lean on the Holy Spirit as your guide.

1. Pray for Family

"The curse of the Lord is in the house of the wicked: but he blesseth the habitation of the just" (Proverbs 3:33). KJV

Pray for your pastor's family and marriage to be blessed. Pray for God to guide your pastor with wisdom on how to prioritize, and how to include plenty of enjoyable times with family.

2. Pray for Strength

"Even the youths shall faint and be weary, and the young men shall utterly fall: But they that wait upon the Lord shall renew their strength; they shall mount up with wings as eagles; they shall run, and not be weary; and they shall walk, and not faint" (Isaiah 40:30-31). KJV

Pray for your pastor to be filled with and remain in the joy of the Lord which is his strength. Pray for physical, spiritual, emotional,and mental strength. Pray for your pastor to get plenty of rest, restoration and refreshment.

3. Pray for Protection

"He that dwelleth in the secret place of the most High shall abide under the shadow of the Almighty" (Psalm 91:1-16). KJV

Pray for a shield of protection from spiritual attacks and from criticism. Pray for pastor's physical health to prosper and for him to be whole.

4. Pray for Prayer Life

"But we will give ourselves continually to prayer, and to the ministry of the word" (Acts 6:4). KJV

Pray for your pastor to have a strong, effective prayer life. Pray for your pastor to have time alone with God meditating on His Word, outside of preparing for sermons. Pray for pastor's personal relationship with the Lord, and his faith to continue to grow and a time of intercession for others. Pray that your pastor will pray faithfully for all of the people who are under his loving care as their pastor. Pray for revelation, wisdom and knowledge, that in all things your pastor will be filled with His peace and joy in thanksgiving.

5. Pray for Direction

"My sheep hear my voice, and I know them, and they follow me:..."(John 10:27). KJV

Pray God will guide your pastor. Pray that your pastor will hear the guiding voice of the Holy Spirit, follow His lead, and obey quickly so he can continue to guide your pastor in paths of light, peace, and truth.

6. Pray Victory Over Temptation

"And lead us not into temptation, but deliver us from evil: For thine is the kingdom, and the power, and the glory, for ever. Amen" (Matthew 6:13). KJV

Pray that your pastor wouldn't be led into any temptation that can't be resisted. Pray for your pastor to remember victory comes by obeying the indwelling Holy Spirit, by knowing and obeying the Word of God. Pray for your pastor to resist the devil by submitting to God so the enemy will flee.

Remember the enemy is pacing to and fro, constantly looking for someone to devour and destroy for lack of knowledge and prayer. The enemy is restless in pursuit.

But your pastor can be restful in pursuit of Christ and his proof will be His peace within. This rest and peace is your pastor's to enjoy through prayer, faith, and obedience to God's commands as well.

7. Pray for Anointing

"The Spirit of the Lord is upon me, because he hath anointed me to preach the gospel to the poor; he hath sent me to heal the brokenhearted, to preach deliverance to the captives, and recovering of sight to the blind, to set at liberty them that are bruised" (Luke 4:18). KJV

Pray for God to anoint your pastor's teaching and preaching, and to prepare receptive hearts for Christ. Pray for the presence of God to be upon him at all times so that Christ's light shines everywhere he goes.

8. Pray for Peace

"And the peace of God, which passeth all understanding, shall keep your hearts and minds through Christ Jesus" (Philippians 4:7). KJV

Pray for the peace of God to rule in the hearts of the pastor and his family at all times.

9. Favor with God and Man

"And Jesus increased in wisdom and stature, and in favor with God and man" (Luke 2:52).

Pray for your pastor to increase in God's wisdom and divine favor with God and man. Pray for open doors to share Christ.

10. Pray for Your Church

" Till we all come in the unity of the faith, and of the knowledge of the Son of God, unto a perfect man, unto the measure of the stature of the fulness of Christ" (Ephesians 4:13-15). KJV

Pray for a supportive and loving church family that will grow in faith and unity. Pray that the church will mature and grow in Christ, with a vision and mission to reach the lost.

11. Pray for Provision

"Give us this day our daily bread" (Matthew 6:11). KJV

Pray for the provision and finances of the Church. Pray for all of the pastor's needs to be met and that he would be blessed. Pray for the church family to have all the provision that they need and they would be blessed as well.

Do you want change anywhere in your life? If so, include more prayer in your days. And please remember: pray for your pastor, as you can change your world through prayer.

A dear friend and faithful minister Joe Walsh, has developed another simple, yet effective strategy for praying for pastors. It goes like this: **He calls it "PDF" which stands for P=Protection, D=Direction, and F=Favor.** This is a wonderful way to pray for your pastor, or anyone else that needs prayer.

I want to encourage you to get ready for a ride of a lifetime in the presence of God. You are about to see God move in your life through your prayers, like never before. He is waiting on you! *Pray*

Pastors Need Prayer

Ted Rose

Chapter 9
Final Prayer
Pass the Mantle of Prayer

**"So he departed thence, and found Elisha the son of
Shaphat, who was plowing with twelve yoke of
oxen before him, and he with the twelfth: and Elijah
passed by him, and cast his mantle upon him"**

(I Kings 19:19). KJV

Here we are at the conclusion of our time of openness in the
presence of God focusing on your role as pastor's prayer
warrior. I would like to thank you for taking time to read this
message. My heartfelt prayer is that God's heart touched
yours with such an impact that the result is an everlasting
blessing, a transformation in you and your pastor.

I have written a prayer for you as you walk this new journey
of daily faith in prayer for your pastor. I pray this will have
an eternal impact on you, the Kingdom of God and your
pastor and family.

Prayer to pass the mantle

Dear Heavenly Father,

I come before your Holy throne to bow before you in prayer.

Father, I ask that You pour out your Holy Spirit to enable everyone reading this book to become people of prayer. Impress upon Your precious children the power that's available through their prayers and precious faith in You.

Please receive them as they enroll in the life-long school of prayer being taught by Your Son, Jesus, for He is the Great Intercessor!

I humbly ask that You would give Your people a sensitive heart toward You and toward the needs of their pastor. Let them know when a crucial moment occurs and emergency prayer is needed.

Use their prayers to quench and deflect the fiery darts of the enemy that are sent to harm or hinder their pastor.

Let each of my praying friends grow deeper in their personal intimacy with You and in intercession for others.

You, Father, are raising up mighty warriors who fight on their knees with the weapon of humility, and I thank You!

Help Your chosen ones to be faithful in their prayer commitment. Strengthen them when their flesh is weak and they are tired and yet prayer is needed.

I thank You for passing Your mantle of prayer to them and making them, walking, talking, breathing, and praying Houses of Prayer everywhere they go from this moment on.

Thank You for answering this special prayer. Please give the God-given mantle of prayer to all those who made this commitment.

May You be glorified, Father!

May the strength of the Father.
The Grace of the Son.
And the Anointing of God's Holy Spirit.
Make this moment a special moment in your life!

In Christ Jesus's name I pray, Amen!

God bless you with His mighty riches that He so generously shares with us. Please know that I will be praying together with you.

Your Brother in Christ,

Ted Rose

Pastors Need Prayer

Chapter 10
A Special Word To Pastors

(LEADERS ONLY)

"But we will give ourselves continually to prayer, and to the ministry of the word" (Acts 6:4). KJV

To my fellow Pastors: I truly pray that the pages of this book have given you encouragement that **help is on the way**. My prayer is that this book will spark a revolution in the church to pray for you and our fellow ministers.

Take a moment and remember back when you first felt the call of God to ministry. Do you remember how in love with the Lord you were? Do you remember how you used to spend hours devouring the word of God, so much so that you didn't even want to put it down. And do you remember the burning passion in your heart to win everyone you could to Christ. When you would have trouble sleeping just wanting to know God's will for your life and His vision for you to reach many souls that were going to hell. But, you wanted to make a real difference in peoples lives.

May I encourage you today to get down on your knees in prayer and rediscover the passion that you once had. Don't let another day go by without a fresh encounter with Jesus. **Cancel your appointments and rearrange your**

schedule if necessary. Do whatever it will take to get alone time, where you pour out your heart and tears without holding anything back. Give to Him your wories, your burdens, your dissappointments, and then let him refresh you with His sweet and powerful anointing and love.

Each of you are in my prayers, even if we haven't met. If you ever need specific prayer, or someone to talk to, then please contact me on the contact info inside the back cover.

Never forget that it is God who has called you, and not man, or you. It is His ministry and He will be there to watch your back and sustain you in your darkest moments.

I would also like to recommend a great resource for you. It is Pastor to Pastor, at **www.ThrivingPastor.org**, a ministry that is within Focus on the Family. Their **Pastoral Care Line number is (877-233-4455)**. Dedicated former experienced pastors are there to receive your call and minister to you with total confidenciallty. Another resource for pastors is **Pastor Serve**, there **crisis phone line for Pastors is (877-918-4746)**. **www.PastorServe.net**.

I love you Pastor and please know that I am praying for you. Never give up, it will all be worth it one day when we will be re-united in Heaven together forever and ever.

Ted Rose

<u>Notes</u>

<u>Notes</u>

<u>Notes</u>

<u>Notes</u>

Ted Rose

To contact Pastor Ted Rose
for a complete list of DVD's, CD's or materials
write:

Pastor Ted Rose
P.O. Box 52
Carmichael, California 95609
Phone: (916) 256-2010

Chairman of the United States National Prayer Council
Chief Intercessor to Rev. Samuel Rodriguez, President of the
NHCLC
Pastor of Prayer at New Season Christian Worship Center

Website: www.USNationalPrayerCouncil.com
Email: Ted@USNationalPrayerCouncil.com

Additional copies of
Pastors Need Prayer
are available at www.PastorsNeedPrayer.com